PIUS XII

by
Ethel Tolansky and
Helena Scott

All booklets are published thanks to the
generous support of the members of the
Catholic Truth Society

CATHOLIC TRUTH SOCIETY
PUBLISHERS TO THE HOLY SEE

CONTENTS

Introduction 3

Early Life and Priesthood 9

Papal Nuncio and Secretary of State 19

Pope at the Outbreak of War 48

Pius and the Plight of the Jews 62

Pius Working Against the Nazis 77

Pius XII - The Post-War Years 88

Bibliography.....................................107

The Authors

Ethel Tolansky, former head of French at the University of Westminster, is currently engaged on research on French Second World War poets, and on the situation of Jews in Tunisia during the Second World War.

Helena Scott is a qualified translator and works as Language Research Coordinator at the University of Westminster.

INTRODUCTION

Pius XII was Pope at a very turbulent period of the twentieth century: from 1939 (he was elected six months before the outbreak of the Second World War) until 1958. Before becoming Pope he had worked in a Roman parish, in the Vatican diplomatic service, in Germany (from the middle of the First World War) and as Secretary of State to Pope Pius XI. During his lifetime he was widely respected and admired, and Christians today can profit from the things he said and wrote, and the example he set with his life.

It is important to know his life and actions, because ever since 1963 people have attacked him, focusing especially on the events of the Second World War, as a way of attacking the Catholic Church. Each of these attacks has been fully answered by people who have studied the facts. But as the attacks are repeated, it is worth getting to know more about the real Pope Pius XII, the holiness of his life, the richness of his contribution to the life and development of the Church, and his concern for the holiness of all. This means looking further than the often-repeated arguments on how he did or did not act during the Second World War.

Pope Pius XII's actions were strikingly consistent throughout his life. For example, during the First World War he organised relief for the victims of war and visited prisoner-of-war camps, and a French prelate, Bishop Fontanelle, said that he did this work so conscientiously that a great number of lives were saved because of him. This very same urgent concern for the welfare of the victims of war was apparent when the Second World War broke out twenty years later. His purpose and motivation were still the same: he had at heart the Church's concern to save souls, and he was naturally also concerned with people's physical, material needs, since he saw them as complete human beings, body and soul.

Major themes

One of the best ways of finding out about a Pope is to read what he wrote. Pius XII wrote an enormous amount, and in the nineteen years of his papacy he published forty-one encyclicals (some short, some very long) as well as composing a huge number of other documents, giving sermons and speeches, sending messages, and writing letters. His encyclicals alone cover a wide range of subjects, and show his deep concern for souls, the way he followed the course of events at every level in different countries around the world, his great love for Our Lady, and the urgency of his prayer for peace. What stands out is his love for God and others, his faithfulness to God's will, and his courage in guiding the Church and defending all those most in need. His writings show how he was fully aware of the dangers of the popular anti-religious ideologies of the time, Fascism, Nazism and Communism, and was tireless in pointing out the truths which were taught by Jesus Christ, and the ways in which those truths applied to current problems and debates.

In the past fifty years Pope Pius XII's achievements have been overshadowed by debate on the period of the Second World War. As well as looking at that period it is also important to recognise that he defended the Church against ideological assaults which were every bit as threatening as air-raids and bombs. His approach was always the positive one of constructing and leading to the truth, rather than a purely defensive one. He was the person most responsible for preparing the Church for the Second Vatican Council - after the Bible, it is Pope Pius XII's writings that are most frequently quoted in the Council documents. He brought about important liturgical changes, and showed an abiding concern for liturgical music. He took steps to promote Biblical studies to ensure that the Church's understanding of revealed truth matured and deepened with the advances in knowledge made possible by the resources of the twentieth century. He was always deeply interested in the technologies of his age, and helped scientists to be aware of the full supernatural dimensions of what they were doing. He saw the role of women in the world as being of crucial importance. He also laid down some major guidelines in the field of medical ethics, which have been valued ever since.

The role of the Pope

In order to understand Pope Pius XII it is important to realise what a Pope is. The papacy is not a political power, and the Pope is not a diplomat. The papacy is a spiritual power (this is much easier to see since the loss of the Papal States in 1870), and the Pope is the father of all Roman Catholics no matter where they are.

Because the Catholic Church is universal, and because the Pope is in touch with members of the Church around the world, Pope Pius XII was more fully aware of what was going on at grass-roots level than any statesman of his time. Priests reported the state of affairs in their parishes to their bishop, and the bishops regularly updated the Pope, who received additional news of each country through the papal nuncio there. This tremendous relationship of communication is part of the structure of the Catholic Church.

All of this can help to explain some of the misunderstandings that have sometimes arisen even among well-meaning historians and journalists when they look at the Pope and his actions. They are used to dealing with the affairs of politicians and statesmen, and they do not understand that the same approach cannot be applied to the Pope, because it leaves out the most important dimensions of his ministry.

A Pope's ministry is a universal service to bring the grace and salvation of God to all those entrusted to him, in and through the Church which is, as Pope Pius himself underlined, the Mystical Body of Christ. To carry out his ministry the Pope may often use diplomatic channels if they are the appropriate ones, but diplomacy is not essential to his role. In particular, during the years Pope Pius XII had spent in Germany as papal nuncio, he had seen the limits of diplomatic efforts and their possibilities. As papal nuncio there, and later on as Pope, he concentrated on stirring up Catholics to a deeper sense of the Church's vision for and of the world. In the first place this meant social justice, so that the people who make up society can receive their rights and have enough sense of responsibility to fulfil their duties towards others, recognising that each person has been created by God and has an immortal soul. When Pope Pius XII put forward very positive, definite ideas on democracy, he did so not as a politician but to show how a society should be run in order to enable people to develop their full capacities in accordance with God's purpose in creating them.

Concern for humanity

Pope Pius XII was a holy man who spoke out fearlessly when necessary, acted courageously after deep thought and prayer to find the most effective path to follow, and inspired many others with his own love for God and the truth. Among all the political turmoil of his times, his great concern was the ultimate vocation of each human being as such, and the ways in which the people of his time acted to develop the life of their souls. This gives us the key to his view of the purpose of his own papacy. When he died in 1958, among many other messages of gratitude and appreciation received by the Vatican was one from Golda Meir, at that time Israel's representative to the UN and later Prime Minister of Israel. She wrote, "We share in the grief of humanity at the passing away of His Holiness, Pope Pius XII. In a generation afflicted by wars and discords, he upheld the highest ideals of peace and compassion. When fearful martyrdom came to our people in the decade of Nazi terror, the voice of the Pope was raised for its victims. The life of our times was enriched by a voice speaking out about great moral truths above the tumult of daily conflict. We mourn a great servant of peace."

EARLY LIFE AND PRIESTHOOD

Early Life

Eugenio Pacelli, the future Pope Pius XII, was born in Rome on 2 March 1876. His parents were devout Catholics, and his mother, Virginia, made a little shrine in her house and took all her children, Giuseppina, Francesco, Eugenio and Elisabetta, to pray there together several times a day. Eugenio grew into a very devout, keenly intelligent boy. He loved to go to the local church, the 'Gesù' which was founded by St Ignatius Loyola (whose tomb it contains), and pray there before the ancient picture of our Lady known as the *"Madonna della Strada"*. Even at this early stage, Eugenio learnt to pray by holding a direct, personal conversation with our Lord and our Lady. When his mother once asked him what he did while he was in the Gesù, he said, "I just tell Our Lady everything." At home he used to play at being a priest and holding church ceremonies. As soon as he was old enough he became one of the altar-servers at the Chiesa Nuova, St Philip Neri's church, which was also close to his home.

As well as being highly intelligent he had an exceptional, even 'photographic' memory. When he was older he could deliver long speeches from memory word-perfect, without having to refer to his notes. As a schoolboy he soon showed a flair for languages, learning Latin and Greek as well as English, French and German. He was a tall, thin boy, who already wore glasses. He was fairly serious, but also lively and well balanced, with many friends. Unselfish and kind-hearted, he never put on airs of superiority because of the high marks he attained for his school work; he was too genuinely interested in the subjects themselves to take credit to himself for doing well in them. He loved playing the violin, and would take it with him on holidays - and fortunately he played it so well that it was a source of pleasure to others too! In due course he specialised in law, and developed a capacity for painstaking work, and a talent for evaluating all the aspects of a question in a serious search for the truth.

In August 1894, at the age of eighteen, he went to do a four-day spiritual retreat. He wanted to see clearly what God was asking him to do with his life. He came home having taken the decision to answer God's call to the priesthood. This sequence of events was to set the pattern for his whole life: he had enormous faith in the power of prayer, and before taking any decision he always prayed about it to implore God's light and help.

None of his family or friends were at all surprised at his decision to become a priest, as Eugenio had always been a serious, devout and gifted person, who seemed suited in every way to the priestly ministry, and generous enough to dedicate himself whole-heartedly to God. In November 1894 he entered the Capranica College in Rome to do his seminary training and study philosophy and theology, for which he attended classes at the Gregorian University. He plunged into the work, and soon every moment of the day was filled with alternating prayer and study. However, his intense dedication took its toll on his health, which had never been very strong, and at the end of the first year he was ordered to go to the country for a complete rest before his health broke down altogether.

Studies

This was a very difficult time for Eugenio: it was clear that he could not carry on at the Capranica College, and he wondered whether it would be possible for him to become a priest, or whether this situation might be a sign that God was not calling him to the priesthood after all. However, some weeks in the country, and the opportunity for deep, tranquil prayer, restored him considerably, and on his superiors' recommendation he spent the next four years living with his family while he completed his studies for the priesthood. He took courses in the history of philosophy, Latin and Greek at the state university of Sapienza, and at the same time followed a course in theology at the Papal Athenaeum of Saint Apollinare, going on to do a doctorate there.

Priest

Before his ordination Eugenio did a retreat during Holy Week, in preparation for the sacrament he was about to receive. He offered himself to God with an open heart and a generous disposition, wanting to seek nothing else in his whole life except God's glory and the good of souls. He was ordained on Easter Sunday, 2 April 1899, at the age of 23, and said his first Mass on the following day in the Borghese Chapel of the Basilica of St Mary Major. He chose this particular chapel for his first Mass because it held the famous picture of "Our Lady, Salvation of the Roman People", and he wanted to dedicate his whole priesthood to Our Lady.

After his ordination he continued studying part-time at the Apollinare, doing an additional doctorate in Canon and Civil Law, and went on to lecture there in law, while he worked as a curate at the Chiesa Nuova, saying Mass, hearing confessions, teaching catechism, going on sick calls and distributing Holy Communion, and doing other pastoral work. Those who knew him said that his whole ambition in life was to continue looking after the spiritual needs of those in the parish. However, in February 1901 he received a visit from Monsignor Gasparri, who worked in the Vatican as Secretary of the Congregation for Extraordinary Ecclesiastical Affairs, which was the equivalent of a Foreign Office. Monsignor Gasparri was looking for assistants in his work, and Don Eugenio

Pacelli had been recommended to him by the Jesuits at the Gregorian University, who had not forgotten him. Don Pacelli was somewhat dismayed by Monsignor Gasparri's request that he should go and work in the Vatican.

"I had hoped to spend all my life on pastoral work," he said. "But all work in the service of the Church is pastoral work," explained Monsignor Gasparri. "Besides, there will still be time for more direct pastoral work as well."

Work in the Vatican

Don Pacelli submitted to this new indication of God's will for him, and started work in the Vatican diplomatic service. Sure enough, he continued to teach catechism, hear Confessions, and occasionally preach at the Chiesa Nuova. He also lectured part-time in canon law at the Apollinare College, gave frequent seminars at a girls' school and was spiritual adviser at a home for working girls. He worked so hard that Gasparri realised he was over-taxing his strength, and told him, "Your lungs need to breathe some fresh air. What's more, we priests talk so much about heaven that it is good for us to feel solid earth under our feet." Accepting the truth of this, Don Pacelli included walking in the open air as part of his daily routine as often as he could, and kept up the habit of taking daily exercise until the end of his life.

Soon after he had started working in the Vatican Queen Victoria died, and Pope Leo XIII appointed Don Pacelli as his envoy to carry his personal condolences to King Edward VII of England. It was not his first journey abroad, for he had already visited France, Belgium, Holland and Germany as a student, but this was a state occasion, and it was Don Pacelli's formal introduction to the world of international diplomacy. His warmth, quick-wittedness and tact made him instantly popular even at that rather solemn gathering.

In 1911 he was to visit England again, this time as part of the Papal delegation to the coronation of King George V.

His reputation at the Vatican was growing, although to begin with he held a very humble post. He built up a vast knowledge of international and legal affairs relating to the Church, and was able to form penetrating and accurate judgements on the basis of his understanding of them. He had a tremendous capacity for sheer hard work, and the drafts and reports he prepared were notable for their clarity and soundness. By the time he had worked there for seven years his reputation had spread abroad: he was offered the post of Professor of Roman Law at the Catholic University of America in Washington. At the Pope's request, however, he declined the offer, though he expressed his sincere gratitude for it both then and later.

His acute mind and legal training were soon employed on the vast project of the codification of canon law, on which he worked with Gasparri, who was now a cardinal. Church laws had been built up over a thousand years of edicts, papal bulls, instructions, decrees, regulations and precedents, each probably useful in context, but unrelated and often contradicting one another. By now there was a vast number of these documents scattered throughout the world, and in such a state of confusion that many church authorities considered it would be absolutely impossible to reduce it all to a straightforward, consistent and intelligible set of laws. Pope Pius X asked Cardinal Gasparri to organise this task, and with the help of Monsignor Eugenio Pacelli, as he now was, all this mass of documentation was collected, worked through, indexed, and put into coherent form as the "Code of Canon Law". The first draft was completed in 1914 and, after due study and revision by the bishops of the Church, it was finally published in 1917.

Despite all his hard work in the Vatican, Monsignor Pacelli still found time for wide-ranging pastoral activity as well. Pope Pius X himself encouraged all priests to work in this sort of apostolate with his writings and his own example. Monsignor Pacelli gave retreats, heard confessions, prepared children for their First Holy Communion, taught a course of philosophy and another of advanced Christian doctrine, and acted as unofficial chaplain to a religious community, the Assumptionist Sisters, together with their pupils and many others.

The First World War

The First World War broke out at the end of July 1914, and on 20 August, heartbroken, Pope Pius X died. His successor was Cardinal della Chiesa, Archbishop of Bologna, who took the name Benedict XV. Monsignor Pacelli was made Secretary of the Congregation for Extraordinary Ecclesiastical Affairs, replacing Cardinal Gasparri who had been made Vatican Secretary of State.

Following the lead given by Pope Pius X, Pope Benedict XV worked endlessly to try and bring the warring countries to a negotiated peace settlement, not discouraged by the unresponsiveness of the governments involved. Nobody who has read anything about the First World War can fail to be horrified by the scale of the killing on the battlefields, most of it for no advantage at all. Pope Benedict suffered immensely, and did not stop appealing to the warring countries to end it. He pointed out in his very first encyclical that thousands of precious lives, especially lives of young men who should have had the future before them, were being wasted for no purpose, but only as a result of their governments' desire for material profit, business interests, and territorial expansion.

Relief work, prisoners of war

At the same time Pope Benedict concerned himself with the victims of the fighting on both sides, since the Vatican was necessarily neutral. He initiated relief work for refugees and those in prisoner-of-war camps, and aimed to facilitate the exchange of letters between prisoners and their families. There were huge numbers of prisoners of war: Allied prisoners captured by the Germans; German prisoners captured by the Russians; and many more on both sides. Pope Benedict made Monsignor Pacelli responsible for the greater part of this work, and he plunged into the task with his usual whole-hearted dedication. He also set up an office to keep track of the names of people who either had been killed, or were missing in action, or had been taken prisoner, so that at least their families were not kept in the agony of suspense unnecessarily. He arranged for priests who spoke the language of the prisoners to visit the camps. They were reminded that no distinctions were to be made between prisoners on the grounds of race, nationality or religion, but all were to be cared for as well as humanly possible.

Between them, Pope Benedict and Monsignor Pacelli managed to open negotiations with all the belligerents for the exchange of wounded or tubercular prisoners and interned civilians. Since these unfortunates were a drain on their captors' resources and could be of no military use to their own countries, the various governments were willing to listen to reason. As a result of these efforts, many thousands of people were able to return to their homes. In addition, the Vatican sent medical supplies to field and base hospitals, and food to the people who had been forced out of their homes as refugees. Monsignor Pacelli organised all this so efficiently that when the Second World War broke out in 1939 the whole organisation was very quickly put into action again.

The war years brought him additional personal sadness, because his father, Filippo, caught influenza at the age of 79 and died on 20 November 1916.

To Germany

Finally, towards the end of 1916, the governments of the Central Powers - the German states and the Austro-Hungarian Empire - indicated that they might be willing to consider a peace plan prepared by the Vatican. The papal nuncio to Bavaria died at about that time, and the Pope ordained Monsignor Pacelli a bishop on 13 May 1917 and sent him to Munich as Archbishop and papal nuncio.

The British envoy to the Holy See, Sir Henry Howard, wrote in his diary that this move "will be a dreadful loss for our British mission to the Vatican, for he is the *one* man who can be trusted implicitly; however, it is also consoling that there should be such an honest man at Munich at present." As for Cardinal Gasparri, he thoroughly agreed that Pacelli was needed for the peace negotiations, and was delighted to see him made a bishop, but he knew he would miss Pacelli's help very much, and his comment was, "They have cut off my right arm."

PAPAL NUNCIO AND SECRETARY OF STATE

The new Archbishop broke his journey to Munich at the shrine of Our Lady of Einsiedeln in Switzerland to ask our Blessed Mother for her special help for his mission, and to pray for peace. He already knew the conditions he would find in Germany, and he took with him huge amounts of food and medical supplies. Although his immediate responsibility was the Pope's proposed peace plan, he was also very concerned to minister to the needs of the ordinary people, who were suffering great hardship as a result of the war, and he started this job by distributing food and medicine to whoever needed it. Meanwhile he limited his own meals to the same amount of food as was allowed by the food-rationing authorities to ordinary citizens.

The situation in Germany was complicated by the fact that each of the German states was semi-autonomous. Officially, Pacelli was papal nuncio to Bavaria, which was ruled by King Ludwig. In practice, since the Vatican had no formal representation in Prussia, which was the most powerful of the states, Pacelli was the point of contact between the Pope and the German Emperor, Kaiser Wilhelm II, as well. To begin with, he brought Pope Benedict's peace plan to King Ludwig, who thought it might succeed, and arranged an audience for him with Kaiser Wilhelm in Berlin.

Working for peace

Here, however, Pacelli's path was not so smooth. After a lengthy audience with the Emperor, and negotiations with the Chancellor, it became clear that the Prussian leaders had no intention of agreeing to the Pope's peace plan, as they were convinced that they could win the war outright. The most Archbishop Pacelli could achieve was obtaining the Kaiser's agreement to stop deporting Belgians to Germany as compulsory labourers. Pacelli, back in Munich after reporting his failure to the Pope, could only leave the eventual outcome entirely in God's hands, and he set to work to get to know the people he was now living among, including both the ordinary people of Bavaria and the diplomats who were accredited to the court of King Ludwig. Most of all he continued his relief work, travelling all over Germany to minister to those in need whether they were homeless refugees or captured soldiers in prisoner-of-war camps. He especially tried to bring help to the children; he said that the sight of those starving, homeless children sent a physical pain through his heart. Everywhere he went he made a deep impression, and the work he did to bring help and comfort to the poor was remembered long after he himself had returned to Rome for good.

Germany finally admitted defeat, and the fighting ended with the Armistice of 11 November 1918. Germany now found itself in a desperate situation, blockaded by the victorious forces until it agreed to make huge payments for war damages. The conditions finally imposed on it by the peace treaty of Versailles in 1919 were felt by Germans to be completely unjust, since they were far harsher than the conditions which had been the basis for the Armistice. The Allies' purpose in imposing these conditions was to prevent Germany from building up the strength to threaten European security again. However, many people stated then and later that the harshness of the conditions imposed could rebound on the Allies who imposed them. Hitler's rise to power was, in this view, largely due to the sense of desperation which the German people experienced. Archbishop Pacelli, a first-hand witness of this part of Germany's development, was to remember this later. As Pope Pius XII, he warned in his radio message of Christmas Eve 1944, when the end of the Second World War was in sight, that "the peace settlement which should be strengthened and made more stable by mutual guarantees... should not give definite countenance to any injustice... and should not impose any perpetual burden."

Communism

Soon much of the German population was on the brink of starvation, and riots and revolution were in the air, with violent attempts by monarchists, nationalists and Communists to gain the upper hand and overthrow the democratic government. The first two of these groups represented elements which had long been present under one form or another, but the ideals of Communism, a relatively recent development, were fast making it clear that it was one of the most dangerous enemies of the Catholic faith. Communism declared that man had no soul and no spiritual life; that God was a myth and the idea of heaven was a fable invented by the powerful to keep the working-classes contented with their lot. Communism stirred up hatred and bitterness to induce people to rebel and claim their basic rights by violent conflict.

In April 1919 Communists seized the Bavarian government and declared Bavaria a separate Communist State. All the diplomats in Munich escaped to Berlin but Pacelli chose to remain behind. The nunciature, where he lived, was once invaded by a small group of German Communists, and once his car was mobbed, but on both occasions Pacelli confronted his attackers and told them that he was there in the service of peace and in the name of God, and they ended up leaving him alone. The following month the Republican German Government regained control of Munich and started hunting down the Communists. When they went to ask Pacelli to help identify the men who had attacked him, he was always 'unavailable'. He was not interested in revenge or victimisation against them.

Fascism

Meanwhile the German Workers' Party was developing, soon to evolve into the National Socialist German Workers' Party, or Nazi Party. In 1920, Clemens August Graf von Galen, the future bishop of Münster and a firm opponent of Nazism until the end, declared that Nazism contained ideas "which no Catholic could accept without denying his faith upon cardinal points of belief." On 1 October 1921, the *Bayerischer Kurier,* a Bavarian newspaper, quoted Nuncio Pacelli as saying: "The Bavarian people are peace-loving. But just as they were seduced during the revolution by alien elements - above all Russians - into the extremes of Bolshevism, so now other non-Bavarian elements of entirely opposite persuasion have likewise thought to make Bavaria their base of operation."

This was Pacelli's first published warning to people about Nazis, but it was not his last. Of the forty-four public speeches that Nuncio Pacelli made on German soil between 1917 and 1929, at least forty contained attacks on National Socialism or Hitler's doctrines. Other Catholic leaders joined him. German bishops solemnly warned the faithful against Nazism on five occasions between 1920 and 1927, explaining that National Socialism was totalitarian, racist, pagan, and anti-Christian.

During these years Pacelli suffered two severe losses: first that of his mother, Virginia Pacelli, who died on 10

February 1920 at the age of 76. Then, early in 1922 Pope Benedict XV died, and Pacelli was as grieved as if it had been his own father. He had always looked on Pope Benedict as his father and teacher during the years they had worked together, and the trust they felt for one another had not lessened during Pacelli's stay in Munich. Pope Benedict was succeeded by Achille Ratti, who had been papal nuncio in Poland and took the name of Pius XI. He and Pacelli were old friends and had considerable respect for each other.

In 1925 Pope Pius XI warned not only against Communism, but against "every political conception which makes society or the State an end in itself, from which naturally, fatally indeed, it finishes in absorbing or destroying private rights." This was at a time when Fascism in Italy and Nazism in Germany were steadily gaining in popularity, and many people were deceived by the promises their leaders made.

Concordats

All this time, Nuncio Pacelli was working to set the relationship between the Catholic Church and the new German 'Weimar Republic' on a sound footing. The legal framework within which the Church operates in each country is established by means of an agreement known as a 'concordat'. This is not a pact between two friendly nations, nor is it a way of extending or centralising Papal power. A concordat is a legal agreement between the Vatican and a nation or state, defining the position of the Catholic Church, its members and its institutions, within that state, and setting out its rights. For instance, a concordat will establish whether a given state will allow, recognise and fund Catholic schools, whether it will recognise weddings performed in a Catholic church as legally valid, who will be the legal owner of Church property and buildings, and so on.

Because the legal set-up, and the situation of the Church, was different in the different German states, it was not possible to draw up one concordat with the whole country. Pacelli started with Bavaria, and after several years of study and negotiation, the concordat was finalised and agreed on in 1924, and ratified by the Bavarian Parliament in January 1925. By this stage Pacelli was officially papal nuncio to Prussia as well as Bavaria, and once the Bavarian concordat was completed he moved from Munich to Berlin. The people of Munich were extremely sorry to see him go, and showered him with letters, speeches and messages of appreciation as he prepared to make his farewells.

Tireless communicator

Pacelli was always capable of recognising and adapting to different circumstances. In Bavaria, which was predominantly Catholic, he was seen first and foremost as the Archbishop he was. In Berlin, for most people he was a diplomat, and his apostolate, his work for the Church, was primarily in the diplomatic field. He never neglected the pastoral work which was his primary responsibility as a priest, but he also threw himself into his diplomatic role. He entertained all sorts of people at the nunciature, from the President, the Chancellor and foreign diplomats, to press reporters, workers and students. He was very popular in many different spheres, having a great deal of personal warmth and charm, quick understanding, openness and sympathy, and a knack of getting on to the wavelength of the person he was talking to. However intense or difficult his workload, he never appeared tired, preoccupied, or uninterested in whoever he was talking to; nor was he ever touchy. People quickly felt at home with him, and far from giving the impression that he was condescending or talking down to them, he showed that he sincerely appreciated their friendship. They also soon learnt that he was as honest and reliable as he was friendly; he never took unfair advantage of something said in confidence, or failed to fulfil a promise or an assurance, however lightly given, unless some unforeseen reason prevented him. He always had time for everybody despite his many commitments. He soon became known as the best-informed diplomat in Berlin, and his views were widely respected.

Another aspect of his work during this time was travelling around the whole country giving speeches and sermons, driven by his love for souls. As well as helping to throw new light or present the Christian perspective on current questions, this enabled him to acquire first-hand knowledge of the whole of Germany and its people, and to be known by them in his turn.

Rise of Hitler

However, all was far from well in Germany. The Nazi party, led by Adolf Hitler, continued to grow in influence, appealing to the masses with its promises to restore German prosperity and its assurance that Germans were a 'master-race', destined to rule the world. Many of the priests and ministers of all the Christian denominations in Germany, not only Catholics, did what they could to warn people against being carried away by such promises and attitudes, but although they had some degree of success they were unable to turn the tide.

Archbishop Pacelli worked hard for four years to finalise a 'Solemn Agreement' which was the Prussian equivalent of a concordat. It was finally ratified by the Prussian government in August 1929. A few months later, in December, Pacelli was recalled to the Vatican to be made a cardinal. He was reluctant to go, considering that his work in Germany was far from complete, particularly in the face of the spread of Nazism. The farewells from the many who knew him in Berlin were an echo of what had happened in Munich in 1925, and when he drove from the nunciature to the station the roads were lined with thousands of people who gave him a warm send-off.

He arrived in Rome at the end of a momentous year for the Papacy: on 11 February 1929 an agreement had been reached between the State of Italy and the Holy See which solved the difficult question of the status of the Vatican as an independent State within Rome, the capital city of Italy. From 1870 onwards, when the Italian Republic had seized the parts of Italy which had been the Papal States, the 'Roman Question', as it was called, had been a constant source of difficulties. Now the jurisdiction of the Papacy was clearly defined and recognised to the satisfaction and delight of both the Holy See and the State of Italy in the 'Lateran Treaty'. One of the Vatican lawyers who had contributed the most to help resolve the whole question was Francesco Pacelli, the new Cardinal's elder brother.

Cardinal Secretary of State at the Vatican

In January 1930 Cardinal Pacelli became Vatican Secretary of State on Cardinal Gasparri's retirement. When Pope Pius XI told him that he was to be Gasparri's successor, Pacelli declared that he felt utterly unfit for that responsible post. The Pope insisted, and Cardinal Pacelli finally said, "Holy Father, I shall do what you wish. But I'm sure that you will be sorry for appointing me." Pope Pius XI smiled, and said simply, "We'll see!"

It was then that Cardinal Pacelli began to become more widely known around the Catholic world. An authority on the Vatican wrote of his courtesy, his intense concentration and devotion when praying, and his love for the liturgy, ending, "I have seen him enter Saint Peter's amidst trumpets, robed in gorgeous vestments; but saying Mass he was transformed into the simple priest with the moving devotion of one profoundly aware of his own unworthiness."

On 29 June 1931 Pope Pius XI issued the encyclical *Non Abbiamo Bisogno* ('We have no need') denouncing the attacks made by Mussolini's Fascists against Catholic Action in Italy. Catholic Action was working to form young boys and girls into good Christians when Mussolini wanted to make them into good Fascists. Because of well-founded fears that Mussolini would act to prevent the encyclical's distribution, the first copies printed by the Vatican Press were entrusted to the American Monsignor Spellman, who took them straight to Paris by aeroplane and publicised the encyclical from there.

Cardinal Pacelli worked with Pope Pius XI for ten years, and there was a deep friendship between the two men although they were of very different temperaments. Pius XI once said, "Cardinal Pacelli speaks with my voice". One of the things Pacelli did to modernise the Vatican of the 1930s was to have a radio station installed inside the Vatican City, which was very soon to prove of crucial importance. As Secretary of State he worked

Cardinal Pacelli in Berlin, 1933.

endlessly, acquiring a thorough knowledge of the situation of the Church around the world. Those were the years of the Depression; the rise of Radical Socialists in Spain, leading up to the Spanish Civil War; Stalin's horrific actions in Russia and the Ukraine; a violently anti-clerical left-wing government in Mexico; and much more.

More trouble in Germany

Cardinal Pacelli was instrumental in drawing up concordats with Austria, Yugoslavia and other nations to provide for the relations between the Catholic Church and the State in those countries. Because Hitler, on becoming Chancellor of Germany, had received dictatorial powers over the whole country and re-written the German constitution, the concordats previously agreed upon with individual German states were no longer operative. In 1933 Cardinal Pacelli negotiated a new concordat with Germany, about which much has been written. Pope Pius XI stated four years later that he had agreed to and signed the concordat "despite many and grave misgivings" because he knew, through Cardinal Pacelli's warnings, that Hitler was most unlikely to keep to its terms; but that he had seen it as the only way of protecting Catholics in Germany. At least the concordat formed a legal basis on which the Vatican could protest when unjust actions were taken against the Catholic Church in Germany and its members. What was more, if the Vatican had rejected this concordat, the Nazis would have said, "We were ready to give the Catholics very favourable conditions and they refused, so we are justified in making things difficult for them now." As Pacelli himself put it, the choice had been between agreement on the terms offered by the Nazi government, or the virtual annihilation of the Catholic Church in Germany.

Concordat with Germany

It is sometimes said that one of the points of this concordat was that Catholics should take no part in politics, and that it signalled the end of the Centre Party, which had been an influential, mainly Catholic political party in Germany. This is very far from the case. The concordat stated that Catholic clergy and religious should not take a hand in party politics, but they were not restricted from making statements about basic human rights; while Catholic lay-people naturally continued to have full freedom to take whatever part they chose in politics provided they were faithful to God's law. The Centre Party itself had collapsed and voluntarily disbanded before the concordat was even signed.

One very important provision of the concordat was that when Jewish people were converted to Christianity and baptised, the German government agreed to regard them as Christians, no longer as Jewish. This would soon mean that Catholic priests were able to help thousands of Jews to escape being arrested and deported to concentration camps by issuing them with baptism certificates, whether or not they were actually baptised.

The total effect of the concordat - at least on paper - was to place the Catholic Church in Germany on an equal footing with the Protestant churches there, with the same rights and privileges.

Nazi breaches of human rights

As Cardinal Pacelli had warned, no sooner had the concordat been signed than the Nazi government began to violate its terms, shutting down Catholic youth groups and Catholic newspapers and printing presses, and closing Catholic schools or turning them into secular schools. Very soon, priests who spoke against the Nazis' increasingly nationalistic and racist measures were being arrested on invented charges ranging from immorality to violation of currency regulations.

The Vatican was especially concerned for human rights in Germany, knowing the Nazi party's vicious anti-Semitism. As soon as Hitler became Chancellor in January 1933, Cardinal Pacelli had instructed the papal nuncio in Berlin to inform the German government of Vatican defence of the Jews, and to warn the Nazis of the dangers of anti-Semitic policies. They took no notice. Many of the laws promulgated by the Nazis were in direct opposition to the teachings of the Church and basic human rights. One was the sterilisation law in July 1933 ordering that Germans who had any physical or mental impairments were to be sterilised so that the 'Aryan race' would be steadily improved. This was soon followed by the Nuremberg laws on German nationality in September 1933, defining on racial lines who was and who was not German. Catholic bishops and priests had already condemned the Nazi belief in race and blood as un-Christian, and they continued to do so. Many were imprisoned and executed for this reason alone. In 1939 the Nazis instituted a euthanasia programme: not content with sterilising "the unfit", people who were mentally or physically handicapped, the government proceeded to collect them in institutions where they were quietly killed, usually by lethal injection. This programme continued operating for years, and even when widespread protests in 1941 caused the Nazi government to declare it had been dropped, it still continued in secret.

Pope Pius XI and his Secretary of State Cardinal Pacelli suffered together over what was happening to everyone in Germany, whether Catholics or not. They both prayed unceasingly for the situation to improve and for the Nazis to realise where their pagan beliefs and inhuman policies were ultimately going to lead them. They warned people clearly of the results of abandoning God and ignoring his laws, which are the laws governing human nature.

Travels abroad, understanding the world

Meanwhile they did not neglect the rest of the world, since they felt the weight of souls and longed to bring them all to God. Pope Pius XI was a strong-minded and sharp-witted man and, first and foremost, a man of faith, and he had great confidence in the abilities of his Secretary of State. He took advantage of several opportunities to send Pacelli to different countries and continents, something which was made easier by Pacelli's gift for languages. This meant that Pacelli had the opportunity to learn about the different countries and their people and situations at first hand; and, of course, the various countries he visited learnt a lot about him.

In October 1934 he was sent to the International Eucharistic Congress in Buenos Aires, Argentina. He spent part of his time on the two-week Atlantic crossing perfecting his Spanish in preparation for the event, in order to be able to speak to people directly as well as give speeches and sermons. Even amidst all the excitement and crowds he never lost sight of the fact that the purpose of the whole occasion was to honour Jesus in the Holy Eucharist, and when he was praying before the Blessed Sacrament he concentrated one hundred per cent on Our Lord. Just seeing him was enough to inspire many other people to do the same. His sermons, as always, were addressed straight to his listeners' hearts, and in the final ceremony of the congress he spoke about peace, trying to make people face the fact that world peace can only be attained if people are at peace with God, if individuals and nations return to Christ and obey his will. This was

something he was to repeat in all sorts of different ways
until the very end of his life. It was not a warning just for
the years leading up to the Second World War, when
everyone realised that conflict was looming. Pacelli (the
name means 'son of peace') repeated it more insistently
still after that war was over. His clear mind, never afraid
to face the facts and always able to see deeply into them,
and above all his sense of the world as God's creation,
gave him a special grasp of the situation underlying day-
to-day events and excitements.

At the close of the International Eucharistic Congress in
Argentina, Cardinal Pacelli visited Brazil, and addressed a
special session of the Brazilian Parliament, this time in
fluent Portuguese. To them, and afterwards to the Supreme
Court in Rio de Janeiro, he spoke about the way man's laws
should relate to God's law, the real meaning of justice, and
the need for a spirit of faith in those who hold authority
over whole countries. Then and on every available
opportunity he spoke out against the enemies of mankind's
basic freedoms - especially the freedom to seek the truth.

Preaching against false philosophies

On 1 April 1935 Pope Pius XI appointed Cardinal Pacelli
as *'Camerlengo',* meaning that in the event of the Pope's
death he would be in charge of making arrangements for
the conclave to elect the next Pope. In that same month
he was saddened by the death of his elder brother

Francesco, to whom he had always been very close. Despite this loss, he went as the Pope's legate to the ceremonies being held at Lourdes from 25 to 28 April to mark the end of the jubilee year for the nineteenth centenary of the Redemption. He used this opportunity to warn the world at large against people who were "denying the fundamental dogma of sin and reject the idea of redemption as injurious to human dignity. With the illusion of extolling new wisdom," he went on, in a clear reference to Nazis and Fascists on one hand and Communists on the other, "they are really only lamentable plagiarists who dress up old errors with new tinsel. They are inspired by a false conception of the world and life. It matters little whether they mass around the flag of social revolution, or are possessed by the superstition of race and blood: their philosophy rests on principles essentially opposed to those of the Christian faith. And the Church does not consent to form a compact with such principles at any price."

Invasions and civil war

Events in Italy continued to point towards war, as Mussolini tried to follow the example set by Hitler in increasing the territory he laid claim to. In October 1935 he ordered the Italian army to invade Ethiopia from what was then known as Italian Somaliland, preferring to listen to Hitler rather than the Pope, who condemned the action as madness. The League of Nations also condemned the invasion, but took no action. By May 1936 Italy was in control of Ethiopia and declared it an Italian colony. It was clear that the more territory Mussolini gained, like Hitler, the more he would want.

In July 1936 came further drastic developments in Europe with the outbreak of civil war in Spain. In the three years it lasted, this war was to cost the lives of many priests, religious, and ordinary faithful, as well as at least equal numbers of those opposed to the Church, as Catholic 'Nationalists' fought Russian-backed 'Republicans' for control of the country.

America

In October 1936 Cardinal Pacelli made a one-month visit to the United States. He was received everywhere with honour and enthusiasm, and the visit enabled him to make an in-depth study of the Church in America. He travelled from one place to another mostly by aeroplane, using the flight time to work on composing his forthcoming speeches and sermons - in English - , and to pray. In this way he covered over eight thousand miles, taking in almost the whole of the United States. At the Catholic University of America he spoke to the lecturers and students about the place of learning in the service of the Church. "God the Creator, who is also the God of supernatural revelation, is the essential and inexhaustible font, embracing and sustaining all things, in which all truth, natural and supernatural, has its source. The Divine Word, who operates in both spheres, speaks to us in different ways in the order of nature and in the order of grace, but the truths of one order can never be found to be in contradiction with the truths and mysteries of the other."

In 1937 Cardinal Pacelli went to France for the consecration and dedication of the new Basilica at Lisieux in Normandy, in the course of a Eucharistic Congress. This was a time of serious worry for Pacelli: his beloved Pope Pius XI was gravely ill, having suffered a heart attack the previous December, and Pacelli appealed to Our Lord, through the intercession of St Thérèse, to restore the Holy Father to health. On the way back he gave a sermon in the Cathedral of Notre Dame in Paris. The well-known French author François Mauriac was among the congregation, and he wrote later, "As the vibrant life of apostolic times can be felt through the very pavement of St Peter's, so we saw the ardent soul of a humble priest through Pacelli's dignity as Cardinal." On his return to Rome, Cardinal Pacelli found to his relief that the Pope had almost fully recovered.

Two Encyclicals

During all this time the persecution of the Catholic Church by the Nazis in Germany was continuing. As Cardinal Pacelli and Pope Pius XI had feared, Hitler had never had any intention of abiding by the terms of the 1933 concordat. Protests were made at every level, and in 1937 Pius XI decided that the time had come to publish to the world what was happening - and to publish it in Germany too, since owing to strict State censorship and police control, it was hard for Germans themselves to find out what was going on in their own country. So that he could not be accused of taking sides in what was becoming an increasingly sharp divide between Fascist-style dictatorships and Communists, the Pope decided to publish at the same time an encyclical explaining why the Church was totally opposed to atheistic Communism. *Mit brennender Sorge* ("With burning concern"), originally published in German, was dated 14 March 1937, and *Divini Redemptoris* ("Of the Divine Redeemer"), on atheistic Communism, was dated five days later, 19 March 1937.

Against Fascism

Mit brennender Sorge had been prepared with the help of Cardinal Pacelli in Rome and Cardinal Faulhaber, Archbishop of Munich, among others. In it, Pope Pius XI made a powerful denunciation of the anti-Semitic Nazi creed of fascism and racism. He said, "Whoever exalts race, or the people, or the State, or a particular form of State, or the depositaries of power, or any other fundamental value of the human community - however necessary and honourable be their function in worldly things - whoever raises these notions above their standard value and divinises them to an idolatrous level, distorts and perverts an order of the world planned and created by God; he is far from the true faith in God and from the concept of life which that faith upholds." He went on, "None but superficial minds could stumble into concepts of a national God, of a national religion; or attempt to lock within the frontiers of a single people, within the narrow limits of a single race, God the Creator of the universe, King and Legislator of all nations, before whose immensity they are 'as a drop of water in a bucket'."

In order to enable the encyclical to reach German Catholics, it was not published in Rome and then sent to Germany, but instead smuggled into Germany without any prior announcement, distributed to all parishes, and read from the pulpits on Palm Sunday, just one week after its publication date.

The Nazi government was quick to retaliate. All the copies that could be found were confiscated and destroyed, people suspected of distributing the encyclical were arrested, and Church publications which reproduced it were banned. Harassment of Catholics and official persecution of the Jews in Germany did not slacken but rather increased. This made Cardinal Pacelli aware of the consequences of denouncing the Nazis' actions and policies publicly - it could make things more difficult for the very people he was trying to help.

The Italian government's reaction to the encyclical was also hostile. Eight months after its publication, Mussolini's Italy joined the anti-Communist axis formed by Germany and Japan in 1936, and on 11 December 1937 Italy formally left the League of Nations.

Against Communism

The other encyclical, *Divini Redemptoris,* published almost simultaneously with *Mit brennender Sorge,* highlighted the false claims of atheistic Communism and materialism. It showed how, while claiming to exist for the sake of the people, atheistic Communism actually reduced the capacities of human nature by denying and forcefully preventing any possibility of access to the supernatural plane, any worship and love of God. It explained that one of Communism's stated goals was to destroy religion, and Communist governments ruled by terror. For these reasons, and because Communism aimed to spread its false teachings by whatever violent or unscrupulous methods it could, the Pope declared that Catholics could not co-operate with Communism in any undertaking whatsoever.

Wars and rumours of wars

In March of the following year, 1938, Hitler moved his troops into Austria unopposed, and announced the *Anschluss* or union of Austria with Germany. The Germans introduced their anti-religious and anti-Semitic laws in Austria, and began to suppress the churches. At the beginning of May, Mussolini welcomed Hitler on a visit to Rome. To show the absolute incompatibility between the worldview shared by Fascists and Nazis, and that of the Church, Pope Pius XI and Cardinal Pacelli moved out of Rome to the Pope's summer residence at Castel Gandolfo before Hitler's arrival, and it was announced that the Vatican Museum with its priceless art treasures, which Hitler had expressed an interest in seeing, would be "closed for repairs" for the duration of his visit.

At the end of the same month Pope Pius XI sent Cardinal Pacelli to Hungary to attend another International Eucharistic Congress in Budapest, from 25 to 30 May. Among his preparations for it, he spent some time studying Hungarian (a notoriously hard language), and he learnt enough to be able to converse at a fairly simple level and to add appropriate greetings in Hungarian to the sermons and speeches he gave in French, German, Italian and Latin.

His words at this Congress were an urgent call to Catholics and non-Catholics alike, appealing to them to realise the vital need this world has of God, and underlining the dangers, only too obvious at that time, which came as a result of denying God and rejecting his law in the name of a false freedom or the delusion of national supremacy. He also warned that there were "too many who, while not actively hostile to Christ, allowed themselves to drift along on the waves of carefree indifference until they were swept away by the current, finally becoming accomplices in the progress of unbelief and the battle against Christ."

He went on, "We should not be surprised that in a world in which the very notion of the fear of God has disappeared, nothing is left but distrust: distrust between husband and wife, between class and class, nation and nation, people and people; a distrust that has risen to such a degree that its brutal force may at any moment explode into a general catastrophe."

It was clear to his hearers that this was a churchman who was very much part of the modern world and fully aware of its dangers as well as its possibilities for good; a man of God who was unafraid to call things by their name and to defy, when necessary, the popular ideologies of the day. His closing words showed how all the threats of the present times could be turned into hope for the future. "All efforts to stave off this calamity will be fruitless unless the spirit of justice and love enters again into the hearts of men and unites them in brotherly love... The Divine Saviour, who promulgated his new commandment, the commandment of brotherly love, at the Last Supper, is now presiding over this Congress as the *King and centre of all hearts*. While his eyes search our eyes, his lips beseech us, repeating once again this immortal word: 'This is my commandment, that you love one another as I have loved you.'"

Persecution increases

On 14 July Mussolini, following Hitler's example, passed laws restricting the civil rights of Italian Jews. However, unlike Germany, Italy had a very small Jewish population and no anti-Semitism. The laws were widely ignored or skirted around, and many Italians went out of their way to display their support for and friendship with their Jewish neighbours. Pope Pius XI protested angrily against the so-called 'Aryan Manifesto' published by the government, branding it a "true form of apostasy" and attacking the extremist nationalism which was in direct contrast with Catholic doctrine. He said, "The spirit of faith must fight against the spirit of separatism and of exaggerated nationalism which are detestable and which, just because they are not Christian, end by not being even human."

In September 1938 came the infamous 'Munich Accord', signed by Neville Chamberlain for Britain, Edouard Daladier for France, Adolf Hitler for Germany and Benito Mussolini for Italy. Hitler had assured the Allies that if he got part of Czechoslovakia (the *"Sudetenland"*, in which a high proportion of the population was of German origin) he would ask for nothing more. Wanting to believe him, and wanting still more to avoid war, the signatories to the Munich Accord agreed that he should annexe the *"Sudetenland"* to Germany. Hitler was encouraged to think that he could expand as he chose, and no-one would really interfere.

On 9 November 1938, Nazis and their sympathisers in Germany rioted against Jews. They attacked homes, shops and businesses belonging to Jews, and set fire to synagogues. Because of all the windows they smashed, the night's events, which had been carefully orchestrated, received the name *"Kristallnacht"* or "Night of broken glass". Many Jewish people were beaten up and even killed by mobs. The whole affair was reported by the authorities as though ordinary German citizens had spontaneously reacted against wicked intruders: the Jewish inhabitants of Germany were represented as the aggressors instead of the victims. Many Jewish people were arrested and sent to concentration camps, and the laws restricting the legal rights of 'non-Aryans' were enforced more and more viciously. Those Jews who were able to emigrate did so, though often only to neighbouring countries.

Pope Pius XI dies

Pope Pius XI and his Secretary of State Cardinal Pacelli were striving all this time to awaken Catholics all over the world to the reality of the situation and the only true solution to it: being converted to God and obeying his laws, living according to the commandments on an individual level and being guided by justice. Like everyone else, they realised that if events continued as they were going, the obvious outcome would be another large-scale war. They knew that a second European war could only be even worse than the one which had ended just twenty years previously. Again and again the Pope offered to mediate between conflicting countries by whatever means possible: conferences, negotiations between two countries, in order to find some just way that would avoid the horrors of war.

11 February 1939 was to be the tenth anniversary of the signing of the Vatican Treaty. A major celebration was planned in St Peter's, and Pope Pius XI prepared a speech in which he would once again try to awaken people's awareness of the only way to true peace. However, he was already old and quite ill. He begged his doctors just to keep him going until 11 February, but in the night of 9 February he suffered a heart attack, and died at 5.30 in the morning of 10 February.

POPE AT THE OUTBREAK OF WAR

The election of Pope Pius XII

The period after the death of a Pope is one of mourning for the whole Church. This sadness was especially acute for Cardinal Pacelli and the others who had been close to Pius XI and loved him. As *Camerlengo,* Pacelli was in charge of making arrangements for the Conclave of cardinals from all over the world who would elect a successor to Pope Pius XI, and he channelled his grief and prayer into the intense work of the next three weeks. The Conclave started on 1 March, and on the following day, his sixty-third birthday, Eugenio Pacelli was elected Pope. He took the name of his predecessor, and became Pius XII.

In electing him, the cardinals had shown that in the situation of the Church and the world of those days they wanted a Pope who was a holy man and a man of prayer; someone who combined deep love for God and his fellow men with wide education and diplomatic experience. They knew that Cardinal Pacelli was a disarmingly warm, open, human individual who could only increase the stature of the papacy in the eyes of the world. In addition, his keen intelligence, his ability to speak languages fluently, and the way people felt instantly attracted to him when they met him on a personal level, were important assets in the role that God, through the cardinals, was calling him to fulfil.

The following day the cardinals gathered in state to present their obedience to the new Pope. Each in turn approached and knelt before him where he sat on the papal throne in the Sistine Chapel. However, when the two oldest cardinals, who were over eighty, came forward, Pope Pius stood up and, before they could kneel, embraced them affectionately, in order to spare them the effort of bending.

He then gave an address which was soon published around the world, speaking more than anything about the need for true and lasting peace. He said, "We invite all men to have peace in their consciences; calm in the friendship of God; to have peace in their families, united and brought into harmony by the sacred love of Christ; and, lastly, to have peace between nations by the interchange of fraternal assistance, by friendly collaboration and cordial understandings, for the sake of the higher interests of the great human family, beneath the eye and protection of Divine Providence. It is in these anxious and difficult hours when so many difficulties seem to oppose the attainment of that peace which is the most profound aspiration of men's hearts, that we raise to the Lord a special prayer for all those on whom rests the high honour and the heavy burden of guiding the peoples in the way of prosperity and progress." This, he said, was the first prayer which issued from the fatherly feeling which God had placed in his heart.

Key helpers

Pius XII appointed Cardinal Maglione as his Secretary of State, with Monsignor Tardini as head of the Vatican 'Foreign Office' or Office of Extraordinary Ecclesiastical Affairs, and Monsignor Montini (later Pope Paul VI) as head of the Office of Ordinary Ecclesiastical Affairs. Cardinal Maglione was to die in August 1944, but Monsignors Tardini and Montini worked with Pope Pius until the end of his life. The four of them made a team of very differing and even opposite characters which was nevertheless strongly united and effective. The relations between Pius XII and Monsignor Montini were much like those of father and son. Monsignor Tardini later wrote a biography of Pope Pius XII, published in Rome in 1959, which showed his deep understanding of and devotion to the man he had served and worked with for so long.

Qualities

Those close to the Vatican respected Pope Pius XII from the start for the outstanding purity of his life, his deep, sincere piety, and his sensitivity. He possessed the qualities of prudence and balance to a remarkable degree, never failing to study a question in depth until he had taken in all aspects of the matter. In conversation he was always humble, natural, and gentle, and he had a great gift for putting people at their ease. He had a quick sense of humour and a loud, ringing laugh; he enjoyed hearing and telling funny stories. He was at home with all kinds of people both high and low, but had a special appreciation for ordinary working people, both in Italy and abroad. He loved to meet them and spend time with them, and he showed his deep concern for them in all sorts of ways, including his constant interests in developments which would improve living conditions for workers around the world, as well as his teaching on justice in social structures. His personal friendliness was balanced by the intense concentration, the total withdrawal into prayer, with which he carried out all religious functions and ceremonies.

In London, Archbishop Godfrey, who was Apostolic Delegate to England, published an article in *The Tablet* on 11 March 1939 about Cardinal Pacelli as he knew him. Among other things, he said that the new Pope was an orator who, "gifted with exceptional powers... spoke with a sincerity and wealth of gesture which told of his own profound realisation of the truths which he explained. One felt that it was the whole man who spoke, that in the midst of his busy life as Secretary of State, the things of God were ever foremost in his mind and were the prop and support which kept him from faltering beneath the burdens of his high office."

Reactions to the election from around the world were generally enthusiastic. People knew that Pacelli was a man of great integrity who would continue the policies, and especially the peace efforts, of Pope Pius XI, and he was seen as a barrier to the spread of Fascism and totalitarianism. Obviously, this very fact made his election unpopular with the Nazis. A Berlin newspaper wrote, "The election of Cardinal Pacelli is not received with favour in Germany because he has always been opposed to Nazism." A Nazi newspaper published the worst insult they could think of: "Pius XI was a half-Jew, for his mother was a Dutch Jewess; but Cardinal Pacelli is a full Jew."

The man and the Pope

One of the things that most struck people who met Pope Pius XII was his combination of deep personal humility with an awareness of the sacredness of the office which he was now called to fill. He was firmly convinced that he was not worthy to be Pope - it was rumoured that after one ballot in the Conclave gave him the necessary majority of votes, he asked for a second ballot in order to give the cardinals the chance to change their minds. He never imposed his own opinion on other people without regard for their views and feelings, but always waited until he was sure that both he and they had the full facts of the case before them and had had time to consider them. He was always available to those who needed him, leaving his private study and work for late at night in order to have time to meet people during the day.

Ever since he was a young priest he had had an enormous reverence and love for the Pope as visible head of the Catholic Church. As Pope himself, he did all he could to make the ceremonies and liturgy in which he took part as beautiful, dignified and, above all, prayerful as possible. He saw this as a way of worshipping God and giving him glory, by dedicating all the riches and splendour of lights and candles, gold vessels, incense, vestments, music and singing, to prayer and praise of God. Throughout his time as Pope he worked to increase this sense of prayerful reverence in the whole of the Church.

Among Pope Pius XII's first actions after his election was to receive the German Ambassador and then the German cardinals in Rome. He wanted to explore any and every possibility of reconciliation between Germany and the other countries in Europe, in a way that would put an end to Hitler's expansionist aggression. The British envoy to the Vatican, Mr Francis d'Arcy Osborne, was pleased at this move and commented to his own government, "I put nothing beyond his powers of achievement!"

Steps to war

Pope Pius XII was solemnly crowned on 12 March. Three days later, Hitler invaded and partitioned Czechoslovakia. At the end of March he turned his full attention to Poland, and demanded that the free city of Danzig (Gdansk) which had many German inhabitants, should belong to

Germany absolutely, and that the Germans should build a
road through the 'Polish Corridor' which separated
Danzig from Germany. The Polish government, with the
tragedy of Czechoslovakia before their eyes, did not
imagine for a moment that if they ceded Gdansk to Hitler,
it would mean the end of his aggression. They refused his
demand, and Britain made a pact with Poland agreeing to
come to Poland's defence if its borders were threatened -
as it was obvious that they soon would be.

On 7 April, Good Friday, Mussolini, following Hitler's
example, invaded Albania, forcing its King, Zog, into exile.

Pope Pius's prayers and efforts for peace were endless.
Throughout the whole of that summer, and particularly in
July and August, he set aside almost every other problem
to concentrate exclusively on working for peace through
all the diplomatic channels available to him. He did not
spare himself, but prayed and worked to save Europe and
the world from the ravages of war. He failed, but his
contribution to the cause of peace against all the odds has
been called the most significant single effort for peace in
the whole of the twentieth century.

A light in the darkness

On 23 August Germany signed a pact with Russia, in
Moscow. War was now virtually inevitable, since Hitler
no longer had to fear the power of Russia if he invaded
Poland. On 24 August Pope Pius made a last appeal for

peace over the radio. He said, "Standing above all public disputes and passions, I speak to all of you, leaders of the nations, in the name of God... I appeal again to governments and their peoples; to governments that they lay aside threats and accusations and try to settle their differences by agreement; to their peoples, that they may be calm and encourage the efforts of their government for peace. It is by force of reason and not by force of arms that justice makes progress. Empires not founded on justice are not blessed by God. Immoral policy is not successful policy... Nothing is lost by peace. Everything may be lost by war... Let men start to negotiate again... I have on my side of the argument the soul of this historic Europe, the child of faith and Christian genius. All humanity wants bread, freedom, justice; not weaponry. Christ made love the heart of his own religion."

World War II - 'Darkness over the Face of the Earth'

Despite Pope Pius's desperate efforts to avert war by inviting the five countries principally involved to a last-minute peace conference, Germany invaded Poland from the west on 1 September 1939, while Russia invaded it soon afterwards from the east. On 3 September, in keeping with its pact with Poland, Britain declared war on Germany. The Second World War had begun.

Pope Pius XII saw clearly the disaster that this represented for Europe, Christianity, and people's lives and souls. He prepared his first encyclical while reports were reaching him almost daily of the atrocities being committed by the Germans invading Poland, and while every prediction was of still worse things to come, since injustice, violence and brutality breed hatred and revenge. The encyclical's Latin title was *Summi Pontificatus* and it is generally referred to in English by the title "Darkness over the Face of the Earth". Despite this name and the terrible situation he was facing, Pius repeated his unfailing hope in God's mercy and in the power of prayer. He described the anguish he felt on looking ahead to all the future harvest of violence and suffering which was being prepared by the events of the present. And yet he said firmly that the appropriate response from the bishop of Rome was prayer, not public condemnation. He identified a lack of Christianity as the basic cause of Europe's present disasters. As visible head of the Catholic Church, he could not contribute political or military strength to help end the war, but he could and would contribute faith and prayer. He believed deeply in the power of prayer to draw down God's mercy, and he knew that God's mercy was all-powerful in its will to redeem mankind even from the worst sins.

The underlying theme of the encyclical was the unity of the human race. The Pope re-stated the fact that the Church, founded by Christ, had to be open to all, with no distinctions on the grounds of race. Specifically, there could be no difference made between Jews and non-Jews, as St Paul had made clear, since Christ had died for all. Pope Pius quoted and emphasised the Letter to the Colossians 3:11, "there is neither Gentile nor Jew, circumcision nor uncircumcision, barbarian nor Scythian, bond nor free. But Christ is all and in all."

He also pointed out the mistaken nature and the catastrophic destiny of the 'Godless State' and deplored the fact that people were forgetting the laws of human solidarity and charity - laws that arise from man's common origin and from the equality of all men's rational nature, whatever nation they belong to. He condemned racists, dictators and those who violated treaties.

The encyclical *Summi Pontificatus* caused a considerable impact around the world, and especially on both sides of the war in Europe. The Nazis were clearly condemned in it, and Heinrich Müller, head of the Gestapo, wrote "This encyclical is directed exclusively against Germany, both in ideology and in regard to the German-Polish dispute. How dangerous it is for our foreign relations as well as our domestic affairs is beyond question."

Pius XII and the Vatican Information Bureau

Composing this encyclical was neither the first nor the only thing Pope Pius did on the outbreak of war. He immediately investigated the need for relief work and had relief projects set in motion, using the systems he himself

had devised during the First World War. The Pontifical
Relief Commission soon had agencies in Norway,
Denmark, France, Belgium, Holland, Greece and
Yugoslavia, and an office was established in Lisbon,
Portugal, to organise the purchase and distribution of
supplies of food and clothing from the United States.
Pope Pius made it clear that he was looking for donations
of money or goods to the Pontifical Relief Commission,
in place of the customary gifts which visitors in peace-
time might bring the Pope.

Using the idea of Benedict XV's organisation for
facilitating correspondence between prisoners of war and
their families, Pope Pius set up the Vatican Information
Bureau to enable people to locate members of their
family who had been deported or imprisoned or had
simply disappeared in the flood of war. Anyone at all
could write to the Bureau with requests for information
on the whereabouts of their loved ones, or giving their
own present address to be passed on, or news of someone
who had been thought lost, and the Bureau carefully
noted every item that arrived and forwarded information
where possible, or filed it for future need. In the whole of
the war and its aftermath over nine million messages
were received and processed (not all from Catholics), and
over thirty-six thousand people were successfully located.
This was an enormously valuable, practical help to the
ordinary people in all countries whom he loved so much.

"If it were only for this work, Pius XII has deserved a monument," wrote a grateful prisoner of war whose family had thought he was dead until the Vatican Information Bureau enabled him to exchange letters with them. And a Professor from Milan who was a prisoner in India wrote, "The Holy See is the only institution which does not forget us."

All this was because Pope Pius felt people's sufferings as his own and wanted to do all he could to help. Out of solidarity with ordinary people, he decided that there should be no heating in the papal apartment, since many people throughout Europe were deprived of any fuel for their homes. He also decided on his own account that he would give up drinking coffee - a considerable sacrifice for an Italian - because in wartime Europe it was simply unavailable to most people.

The Polish Bishops

Many people strongly urged the Pope to speak out and condemn the Nazis. The Allies wanted him to do so because it would help their war effort to be able to use his words in their propaganda. In the case of the Nazi atrocities in occupied Poland, the exiled Polish bishops Radonski and Hlond, and President Raczkiewicz, in exile in London and in France, told him repeatedly that Catholics in Poland felt that the Pope had abandoned them to their fate, and had even struck a deal with the Nazi invaders. Archbishop (later Cardinal) Sapieha of Kraków, from inside Poland, had originally also asked the Pope to speak out. But, learning from bitter experience, he asked the Pope *not* to speak publicly, as it would only make matters worse. In November 1942 he wrote to the Pope, "We much deplore that we cannot communicate Your Holiness's letters to the faithful, but they would provide a pretext for fresh persecution, and we already have those who are victims because they were suspected of being in secret communication with the Holy See." Pope Pius could see the justice of this. He wrote to the bishops in Poland, but left it up to them to make his words public or not.

Bishop Radonski was a Polish bishop who had been out of Poland at the time of the German invasion and had been refused re-entry. He spent most of the war in London. He asked the Pope repeatedly for explicit condemnation of the German atrocities against the Poles. Cardinal Maglione, Papal Secretary of State, wrote to Bishop Radonski on 9 January 1943, and explained why the Pope's words of encouragement and consolation to the Polish bishops had not been published. "If you ask why the documents sent by the Pontiff to the Polish bishops have not as yet been made public, it is because it seems better in the Vatican to follow the same norms as the Bishops themselves observe. As is known, they have not made these documents public so that the sheep confided to their care do not become victims of new and still fiercer persecutions. Is not this the right thing to do? Or should the father of Christianity increase the misfortunes suffered by the Poles in their own country?"

On 18 May 1942, drafting a possible response from the Pope to a message from Archbishop Sapieha about the dreadful conditions in occupied Poland, Monsignor Tardini noted that two things were necessary: first, to support the morale of the Polish bishops and especially that of the Archbishop of Kraków; and then to offer encouragement to the Polish people by showing them that the Holy See is the defender of inviolable Christian and human rights. The first objective seemed rather easy to accomplish; the second much less so. Was it necessary to issue a solemn protest before the world? Tardini rejected a display of this kind, not that there was no basis for such a protest, nor that a public condemnation did not fall within the prerogatives of the Holy See, "which is likewise the protector of natural law". And yet, "in present circumstances a public condemnation by the Holy See would largely be exploited for gain by the parties engaged in the conflict. Furthermore, the German government, feeling itself chastised by this, would undoubtedly do two things: it would increase its persecution of Catholicism in Poland, and it would use every means to hinder the Holy See from having contact with the Polish episcopacy and from performing its works of charity, which for the moment it can still carry out although in a limited way. And so a public statement from the Holy See would surely be perverted and exploited for the purposes of persecution."

PIUS AND THE PLIGHT OF THE JEWS

During the war it is clear that Pius XII deliberately avoided mentioning Jews (except in quotations, as in *Summi Pontificatus* quoted above), or naming Nazis specifically, in public. The main reason for this policy has often been stated. To denounce the Nazis for their persecution and massacre of the Jews would have provoked furious retaliation, which would have been directed not against himself, or not only against himself, but against the Jews. Pius XII knew a lot about Hitler and the Nazis, and his understanding of their reactions deepened with experience. One of the people who have studied Pius XII's life in depth writes, "He knew that Hitler was a pathologically obsessed anti-Semite. Whenever the word 'Jew' was mentioned in his presence, he flew into a rage and intensified the criminal persecution of the Jews. In such circumstances, a responsible leader thinks before he speaks, and does not simply go ahead saying 'Let wisdom be damned' and cause an explosion." At the Nuremberg trials after the war, Ernst von Weizsäcker, Germany's Chief Secretary of Foreign Affairs until 1943 and then Ambassador to the Holy See, testified: "It was well known - everybody knew it - that the Jewish question was a sore point as far as Hitler was concerned. To speak of interventions and requests submitted from abroad, requests for moderation of the course taken: the results of these, almost in all cases, caused the measures to be made more aggravated, and even more serious, in effect."

Levels of protest

In an address on 2 June 1943, the Pope explained that "Each of the words we address to the competent authority on this subject, and all our public utterances, have to be carefully weighed and measured by us in the interests of the victims themselves, lest, contrary to our intentions, we make their situation worse and harder to bear." He went on, "The ameliorations apparently obtained do not match the scope of the Church's maternal solicitude on behalf of the particular groups that are suffering the most appalling fate. The Vicar of Christ, who asked for no more than pity and a sincere return to elementary standards of justice and humanity, then found himself facing a door that no key would open."

He did not find this an easy course to take but was convinced that it was the best one. On 20 February 1941 he had already written, "When the Pope wanted to cry aloud in a strong voice, waiting and silence were unhappily often imposed; when he wanted to help and to bring aid, patience and expectation [were required]." He repeated the same thing on 3 March 1944: "Frequently it is with pain and difficulty that a decision is made as to what the situation demands: prudent reserve and silence or, on the contrary, candid speech and vigorous action."

The arguments which weighed with the Pope and his helpers about how to respond to the situation in Poland applied equally, or even more so, to the sufferings of the Jews, because they were dealing with the same people: the Nazis. According to Robert Kempner, the American deputy chief of the Nuremberg war crimes tribunal, "Any propaganda attempts undertaken by the Catholic Church against Hitler's Reich would not only have been a provoked suicide; but would have hastened the execution of still more Jews and Catholic priests."

A Jewish man who was sheltered by Catholics during the German occupation of Rome from September 1943 to June 1944 said later, "None of us wanted the Pope to speak out openly. We were all fugitives, and we did not want to be pointed out as such. The Gestapo would only have increased and intensified its inquisition.... It was much better the Pope kept silent. We all felt the same, and today we still believe that."

Albrecht von Kessel, aide to Ernst von Weizsäcker testified at the Nuremberg war crimes trials: "I am convinced, therefore, that His Holiness the Pope did, day and night, think of a manner in which he could help the unfortunate Jews in Rome. If he did not lodge a protest, then it was [...] because he thought, justifiably, that if he protested Hitler would go crazy. And that would not help the Jews at all, that would give one the justified fear that they would be killed even more quickly. Apart from that, the SS would probably have been instructed to penetrate into the Vatican and lay hands on the Pope." A very real danger existed at that stage that the Nazis would invade Vatican territory; and this, of course, would have meant not only imprisonment and possible death for the Catholics, but certain death for all the Jewish people whom they were sheltering.

Twenty years later, on 6 April 1963 in *Die Welt,* von Kessel wrote: "We were convinced that a fiery protest by Pope Pius XII against the persecutions of the Jews would in all probability have put the Pope himself and the Curia into extreme danger but [...] would certainly not have saved the life of a single Jew. Hitler, like a trapped beast, would react to any menace that he felt directed at him, with cruel violence."

The Chief Rabbi of Denmark, Marcus Melchior, who managed to escape the Nazis with the help of Catholics, said, "If the Pope had spoken out, Hitler would have probably massacred more than six million Jews and perhaps ten times ten million Catholics, if he had the power to do so."

The Pope himself had said in a private conversation in 1942, "No doubt a solemn protest would have gained me the praise and respect of the civilised world, but it would have brought to the poor Jews an implacable suffering, even greater than the one they are now suffering." He could have spoken out boldly, condemning Hitler by name for persecuting and killing Jews and other named groups. He was well aware that this would have resulted, briefly, in his being praised for playing the hero, and he could have won public acclaim for his courage. He was also fully aware that the most certain result would have been furious reprisals.

Level of reprisals

Nazi reprisals were not mere threats and not slight: they were appalling. They were a central part of Nazi repression in all occupied countries. Among the most notorious instances were the complete obliteration of the Czech village of Lidice (as well as widespread killings throughout the whole country) on 10 June 1942 after the assassination of Reinhard Heydrich, and the Ardeatine Caves massacre of as many as 335 prisoners in Rome after a bomb attack by Communists) had killed thirty-five German soldiers on 23 March 1944 in the Via Rasella. These are just examples: there were many, many more instances.

Most telling of all perhaps was the consequence of the Catholic bishops' public denunciation in occupied Holland of German deportations of Jews on 26 July, 1942. In retaliation for the bishops' protest, the Nazis in Holland announced that Jews who had converted to Catholicism were no longer exempted from deportation; they were rounded up within the next two weeks and deported. One of the victims of this round-up was St Teresa Benedicta a Cruce (Edith) Stein. In the end, 79% of the total Jewish population of Holland disappeared into the death camps, a higher proportion than in any other Western country.

The policy of the International Red Cross was the same as the Pope's, and for the same reasons: actions, not public protests. The International Red Cross was also criticised for this, after the War, by people who did not appreciate what the real situation had been.

Radio messages

Throughout the war the pope's radio messages were of great importance in keeping up the morale of Catholics and helping people of goodwill all over Europe to recognise their responsibilities in the circumstances of war. As he said plainly in a broadcast in November 1939, "when Catholics are not aware of their duty with regard to the non-Catholics throughout the world, this is a defect of their Catholic mentality."

In the first place, Pope Pius made sure that everyone on both sides (and this included Catholics on the Axis side) knew quite clearly what the teaching of the Church was concerning the Nazi doctrines of racial superiority. He reminded them endlessly, just in case they needed reminding, that all men are equal, created equally by God; and that injustice and murder were never permissible. Pius XI had said, famously, in 1938, "For Christians, anti-Semitism is unacceptable. Spiritually, we are all Semites," referring to the fact that Abraham is "our father in faith". Pius XII in turn made it totally clear that co-operation with the Nazi racial agenda and Jewish persecution could not be allowed. No Catholic could pretend not to know that this was the teaching of the Church. In the encyclical *Mystici Corporis,* as in the previous one *Mit brennender Sorge,* Nazi ideology was clearly condemned for anyone who chose to heed. Far too many German Catholics, however, out of either ideological agreement or well-founded fear of persecution, chose instead to follow the nationalistic goals of their government rather than listen to the entreaties of the Popes. (In their defence, it has to be said that for years they had been subjected to a constant stream of viciously misleading propaganda against the Church and the clergy, while the Vatican Radio broadcasts and other sources of accurate information were being blocked and censored on a massive scale. This was one of the problems which the Pope and the German bishops had to try and cope with.)

In his Christmas addresses, which he knew would be most widely and easily circulated, Pope Pius made it clear what was going on. In particular, in the address for Christmas 1942, he expressed his hope that the fighting would come to an end for the sake of all the victims of war - combatants, widows and orphans, and exiles. "Humanity owes this to the hundreds of thousands of people who, without any fault of their own and sometimes because of their nationality or race alone, have been doomed to death or to progressive extermination." This was understood by both sides, gratefully received by those under occupation, and roundly condemned by the Nazi leadership as a breach of Vatican neutrality. The Allies had thousands of copies of this message dropped over Germany from aeroplanes. The Nazis were furious with the message: one of the leading Nazis said on 22 January 1943 that "The Pope has denounced the National Socialist new European order. His speech is one long attack on everything we stand for. He says that 'God regards all peoples and races as worthy of the same consideration': here he is clearly speaking on behalf of the Jews. He virtually accuses the German people of injustice towards the Jews, and he makes himself the mouthpiece of the Jewish war criminals."

On 2 June 1943 in an address to the cardinals which was broadcast on Vatican Radio and clandestinely distributed in printed form within Poland, the Pope expressed in new and clear terms his compassion and affection for the Polish people and predicted the rebirth of Poland. "No one familiar with the history of Christian Europe can ignore or forget the saints and heroes of Poland... nor how the faithful people of that land have contributed throughout history to the development and conservation of Christian Europe. For this people so harshly tried, and others, who together have been forced to drink the bitter chalice of war today, may a new future dawn worthy of their legitimate aspirations in the depths of their sufferings, in a Europe based anew on Christian foundations."

The Vatican Radio was used by Pius XII to amplify and in some cases make more specific what he wanted to say. On 21 January 1940 the radio station broadcast, not only in German but in other languages as well, a description and denunciation of German policy in Poland. The announcer stated: "Conditions of religious, political and economic life have thrown the Polish people, especially in those areas occupied by Germany, into a state of terror, of degradation, and, we dare say, of barbarism... The Germans employ the same methods, perhaps even worse, as those used by the Soviets... Still more violent and constant are the attacks upon justice and the most elementary decency in sections of Poland that have fallen under German control."

At other points Vatican Radio announced, "He who makes a distinction between Jews and other men is unfaithful to God and in conflict with God's commands."

And again, "The life and activities of all must be protected against arbitrary human action. This means that no man has any right on the life and freedom of other men. Authority... cannot be at the service of any arbitrary power. Herein lies the essential difference between tyranny and true usefulness... The Pope condemns those who dare to place the fortunes of whole nations in the hands of one man alone, a man who as such is the prey of passions, error and dreams."

These are just a few instances. Through messages like these issued over the radio, Pope Pius showed clearly where the Nazi ideology was wrong, and why. He never ceased to remind anyone who could listen to or read his words of what the Church taught as the charity of Christ, and what was being done in direct contrast with that charity. As a result of his words, Jewish individuals and organisations knew that they could turn to him for help; and they did, throughout the war. What is more, the influence of the Pope's words was acknowledged with respect and gratitude throughout the free world. In December 1940 the famous physicist Albert Einstein, who was a Jewish agnostic and had fled from Germany to America, wrote in an article in *Time* magazine, "Being a lover of freedom, when the Nazi revolution came in Germany, I looked to the universities to defend freedom, knowing that they had always boasted of their devotion to the cause of truth; but no, the universities immediately were silenced. Then I looked to the great editors of the newspapers, whose flaming editorials in days gone by had proclaimed their love of freedom; but they, like the universities, were silenced in a few short weeks. Only the Catholic Church stood squarely across the path of Hitler's campaign for suppressing the truth. I never had any special interest in the Church before, but now I feel a great affection and admiration because the Church alone has had the courage and persistence to stand for intellectual truth and moral freedom. I am forced thus to confess that what I once despised, I now praise unreservedly."

What Pope Pius did

While avoiding any public mention of the Jews and their plight, Pope Pius worked constantly to save them by whatever means he could. One was the Catholic refugee committee in Rome. It has been reported that this committee enabled thousands of European Jews to enter the United States, providing them with efficient documentation including baptismal certificates, visas, their fares, and financial aid. The baptismal certificates were of crucial importance. During the Second World War they were freely given to Jews, to enable them to apply for emigration and immigration as Christians, not Jews, under the various Concordats; they thus by-passed the quotas on Jewish immigration imposed by many countries, including Britain and the U.S. It should perhaps be pointed out that actually being baptised was not a requisite for receiving one: those who distributed them were quite clear about the need expressed by Pope Pius when he instructed one of his nuncios "to save lives by every possible means."

Clandestine help

The story of the diplomatic and other negotiations made by Pope Pius time after time, country after country, in response to appeals for help for Jewish people, or news of recent or impending attacks, has been carefully documented in many books and articles. He gave detailed instructions to his envoys, the nuncios or the bishops of each country concerned, on the actions they should take in order to halt, delay, or mitigate in any way possible the process of persecution and deportation. One Jewish family could be taken off a transport here; one group of Jewish people could be exempted from deportation there; one particular round-up could be delayed for a few days in a particular town, giving at least some Jews the opportunity to escape or find shelter; one man could be released from a concentration camp on legal grounds and sent to a neutral country. Pope Pius continued this work from the beginning of the war until the end. It has been reliably estimated that the Catholic Church can be reckoned to have saved at least 700,000 and more likely as many as 860,000 Jews from death, in the whole of the war. In relation to the numbers killed this figure is very small - and Pius himself was very conscious of this fact, saying to someone who brought him the thanks of Grand Rabbi Isaac Halevi Herzog after the war, "I only wish I could have done more."

A large part of the Vatican's relief effort was directed to providing money to enable Jewish people to leave Europe and get to the United States, Central or South America, or any other possible country. Pope Pius gave all the money he could raise for this purpose, including his personal fortune.

Sheltering Jews

As is well known, Pope Pius encouraged all Catholics and especially priests and religious, to help and shelter Jews. Throughout occupied Europe, although they themselves were in difficulties, and were endangering themselves by their actions, Catholics as well as many others, Christians or not, provided heroic help to Jews, helping them to hide or escape. This story is one that has often been told, and many more instances are still being discovered. Of course they did not wait to be told what to do by the Pope; but they knew that they had the Pope's moral authority, support and encouragement for their efforts.

In particular, when the Germans took control in Italy after the Italian government surrendered to the Allies in September 1943, Pius lifted the obligation of 'enclosure' for cloistered monks and nuns in Italy and instructed them to open their doors to Jews and shelter them for as long as necessary, in secret. This saved many thousands of Jews from deportation and death.

He himself sheltered thousands of Jews and other refugees in the Vatican itself and in Castel Gandolfo, the papal summer residence outside Rome. 'Sheltered' included feeding them - with Kosher food - and providing for them in every way refugees could need.

One episode which has caused a lot of controversy is the round-up of Jews in Rome on 16 October 1943. The Nazis had occupied Rome after the fall of Mussolini in July 1943. At the end of September, the Nazi governor summoned the leaders of the Jewish community of Rome and announced that unless they paid the Nazis a large ransom in cash and gold within three days, two hundred Jews would be arrested and sent to concentration camps - which, as everyone knew by that time, meant that they would never be heard of again. The Jewish people of Rome raised a certain amount of the ransom, but could not manage to find the full sum demanded before the deadline. They appealed for help to the Pope, who promptly assured them that he would supply the balance needed, and the ransom was paid.

However, the Nazis had never had any intention of leaving the Jewish population of Rome in peace. The payment of the ransom merely gave the Jews (and the Pope on their behalf) a false sense of security, which was horribly shattered in the morning of 16 October by the news that a Nazi raid during the night had netted more than one thousand Jewish people, who had been taken away in trucks.

Cardinal Maglione, on the Pope's behalf, summoned Ernst von Weizsäcker, the German Ambassador to the Holy See, to the Vatican. Although officially a Nazi representative, von Weizsäcker sympathised with the Vatican and with the Jewish victims of the Nazis. He was ashamed and appalled at the news of the round-up, but when Cardinal Maglione asked him to relay a strongly-worded protest from the Vatican to his government, with the demand that the arrests of Jews should be halted immediately, he replied that he thought such a protest, as almost always, would have the opposite effect. He begged Maglione to allow him to handle things his own way. Cardinal Maglione agreed. Von Weizsäcker sent his government two telegrams, saying that the Pope was so anxious to preserve Vatican neutrality that he did not wish to make any protest about the arrests of Jewish people, even though these arrests had been made under his very windows. In this way, von Weizsäcker avoided inflaming Hitler's anger against the Jews of Rome or against the Vatican, since there was, he considered, a real danger that otherwise Hitler might give the arresting of Roman Jews his personal attention and also order a direct attack on the Vatican. At the same time von Weizsäcker convinced the Nazi governor of Rome that the arrests of Jews were causing considerable disaffection among the Italian population, and were also diverting the energies of soldiers who were more urgently needed for the war effort against the advancing Allies. The result was that, although the Nazis had originally intended to deport the whole Jewish population of Rome to concentration camps, there were no further round-ups in Rome. Carlo Sestieri, a well-known Roman Jew who was hidden in one of the Vatican buildings while his wife was protected in a nearby convent, said afterwards, "Thousands of Roman Jews would have been captured by the Nazi troops after 16 October 1943 had it not been for the prudent politics of the Vatican.... Perhaps only the Jews who were persecuted understand why the Holy Father, Pope Pius XII, could not publicly denounce the Nazi-Fascist government.... Without doubt, it helped to avoid worse disasters." (Fortunately, Weizsäcker's telegrams misled his Nazi superiors as he intended. Unfortunately, they also misled certain historians later, who took them at face value.)

PIUS WORKING AGAINST THE NAZIS

There is a widely-held idea that Pius favoured the Nazis because he was obsessed with the danger of Communism, and he wanted the Nazis to win the war to prevent Europe being taken over by Communists. This is quite contrary to the truth. In fact, he actually co-operated with several German resistance attempts to overthrow Hitler from early in the war. The first one was at the end of 1939 and the beginning of 1940. A group of conspirators from the German High Command and the German Intelligence service, including Colonel Hans Oster, General Ludwig Beck, and Major Hans Dohnanyi, wanted to overthrow Hitler, but needed assurance from the Allies beforehand that they would actually proceed to a negotiated peace once Hitler had gone, rather than taking advantage of the situation to occupy Germany and treat it as a defeated nation. They sent a Catholic, Dr. Josef Müller, to the Vatican to ask if the Pope would forward their proposals to the Allies. Pius agreed immediately that "the German opposition must be heard in Britain," and arranged to relay messages between Müller and Francis d'Arcy Osborne, British envoy to the Holy See, so that he could forward them to his government. However, in the end the proposals were rejected by Britain as unlikely to succeed. On several occasions Müller also brought messages to Pius from sources inside Germany concerning military plans and movements. Owen Chadwick, a British historian who has made a special study of the Vatican at this period, concluded that never in all history had a Pope engaged so delicately in a conspiracy to overthrow a tyrant by force.

Communist Russia

There was also the question of extending the American lend-lease scheme to Russia in 1941. Hitler had suddenly attacked and invaded his ally, the Soviet Union. As a result, the Soviet Union applied to be included in the Atlantic Charter and became in effect one of the Allies. *Divini Redemptoris,* Pope Pius XI's famous encyclical condemning Communism, had declared that no Catholic should co-operate with Communism in any way. American Catholics felt this probably meant they should oppose the lend-lease scheme for Russia. President Roosevelt applied to Pius XII for clarification, and the Pope declared that it was the Russian people who had been attacked and invaded by Hitler, and helping them was not the same as helping Communism. The Vatican issued a statement to be read out by American Catholic bishops which said, "The attitude of the Holy See with regard to the Communist doctrine is and remains what it always has been. However, the Holy See has nothing whatsoever against the Russian *people*. It is now the Russian people which has been unjustly attacked and is suffering greatly as a consequence of this unjust war. This being so, Catholics should not have any objections to collaborating with the United States government to help the Russian people by giving the latter such assistance as they need."

In addition, Pius agreed not to denounce Soviet atrocities since such denunciations would be used as propaganda by the Axis powers. This cost him a great effort, and he wrote to Myron Taylor, Roosevelt's personal representative to the Pope, "At the request of President Roosevelt, the Vatican has ceased all mention of the Communist regime. But this silence, that weighs heavily on our conscience, is misunderstood by the Soviet leaders who continue the persecution against churches and faithful. God grant that the free world will not one day regret my silence."

In other words, he maintained that the first thing to do was get rid of the Nazis, not because the Communists were less harmful to free societies in the long run - he was quite clear about that - but because the actions of the Nazis had to be stopped, urgently, at all costs.

Teaching the truth - Three more Encyclicals

As visible head of the Church and representative of Christ on earth, Pope Pius was conscious of his responsibility to teach and spread the truths on which the moral law and practice of the Catholic Church is based. In particular, he felt that if Catholics themselves understood Christ's mind and teachings more deeply, they would be able to counteract the violence and hatred spread on all sides by the war, and, basing their own behaviour on the love and grace of God, work effectively to bring about a just and lasting peace.

Accordingly, the Pope prepared an encyclical, *Mystici Corporis,* on the Church as the Mystical Body of Christ. It was completed and finally published on 29 June 1943. The Pope explained how it applied to the circumstances of that time, but the encyclical is equally relevant today, as its teaching is, of course, timeless.

In it, the Pope reflected on the divine and human natures of Christ and on his infinite love for mankind. Then he showed how this love was expressed in founding the Church. "It was possible for Him to impart these graces to mankind directly; but He willed to do so only through a visible Church made up of human beings, so that through her all might co-operate with Him in dispensing the graces of Redemption."

The Pope described the place of the Sacraments in the work of our redemption, and emphasised the way God is always ready to forgive even the worst sins as long as we are genuinely sorry for them, and do not cut ourselves off from the Church through which God's forgiveness reaches us. He explained exactly why the Church is called not just a 'body' but "the mystical Body *of Christ*". He underlined the fact that we are all organically united to Christ and to one another in Christ. And he said that if Christ is the head of this Body, the Holy Spirit is its soul, and is the source of the Church's unity in Christ. His view of the Church was not inward-looking but open to all, since, as he said, "Christ, by his blood, made the Jews and Gentiles one, 'breaking down the middle wall of partition... in his flesh' by which the two peoples were divided."

The encyclical also explains that "It is the will of Jesus Christ that the whole body of the Church, no less than the individual members, should resemble him." The Pope explained how the Church can and should resemble Christ in all that she does. This is because Christ "so sustains the Church, and so in a certain sense lives in the Church, that she is, as it were, another Christ." He went on to clarify that this does not mean that the Church, like Jesus himself, is of one divine nature with God the Father; but that Christ gives his life not only for the Church but to the Church.

The Pope also wanted to make it clear why "if at times there appears in the Church something that indicates the weakness of our human nature, it should not be attributed to her juridical constitution, but rather to that regrettable inclination to evil found in each individual, which its Divine Founder permits even at times in the most exalted members of His Mystical Body, for the purpose of testing the virtue of the Shepherds no less than of the flocks, and that all may increase the merit of their Christian faith. For, as we said above, Christ did not wish to exclude sinners from His Church; hence if some of her members are suffering from spiritual maladies, that is no reason why we should lessen our love for the Church, but rather a reason why we should increase our devotion to her members." And he went on to spell out the lesson: "But, corresponding to this love of God and of Christ, there must be love of the neighbour. How can we claim to love the Divine Redeemer, if we hate those whom he has redeemed with his precious blood, so that he might make them members of his mystical Body? For that reason the beloved disciple has warned us: 'If any man say: "I love God", and hates his brother, he is a liar. For he that loveth not his brother whom he seeth, how can he love God whom he seeth not? And this commandment we have from God, that he who loveth God loveth his brother also' (*1 John* 4:20-21)."

The Pope completed the teaching of this encyclical with another, published on 30 September of that same year, called *Divino Afflante Spiritu,* ('Inspired by the Divine Spirit') which set out to promote Biblical studies as the necessary means for a deeper and truer understanding of God's revelation to mankind. After the war, he was to write his longest encyclical *Mediator Dei* ('Mediator of God') on all aspects of the Church's liturgy, as the prayer of the Mystical Body offered to God.

All this was because, as he had said so often and was to repeat tirelessly, it is only the truth of Christ that can save mankind from destruction. Systems of government and social order that are genuinely based on Christian principles can achieve lasting peace and real social advancement; those that are based on false and mistaken theories only lead to disaster, even if they appear successful in the short term.

Our Lady's help

Pope Pius had enormous trust in Our Lady and the power of her intercession before God. On 13 May 1942, the silver jubilee of his ordination as a bishop, he had dedicated the whole human race to Mary's Immaculate Heart, assigning a special feast day in honour of the Queenship of Mary. He himself never stopped appealing to her to restore peace and justice to the world.

Hard work

How did Pope Pius manage to accomplish all that he did during the war? His diplomatic efforts on behalf of the Jews, both official, semi-official and unofficial; his organisation of relief work; his personal attention to all the many appeals for help that reached him; his sermons, speeches and radio addresses; his audiences, both large and small, which continued throughout the war; his thorough grasp of the rapidly-changing situation in Europe and around the world; his encyclicals; and not least the generous amount of time he gave to prayer and devotions: all this seems impossible for one man to have found the time and energy for.

Pope Pius knew how to delegate work to the right people, and his helpers in the Vatican functioned well as a team. He himself had always been known for his capacity for work, and now, with so much depending on him, he gave himself no respite and took no holidays. He was helped by his phenomenal memory and the habit he had perfected of organising his work rationally and using every available second. He normally worked very late into the night, or even into the early hours of the morning. It would be wrong, however, to think of him as a 'workaholic', because he always gave each aspect of his day its correct priority, including the time he spent taking exercise in order to maintain his health, which he did successfully. What enabled him to keep going was his love for God and for souls.

The final years of the war

The Germans occupied Rome from September 1943 to the beginning of June 1944. As the Allies moved closer to Rome during this period, there was every possibility that Rome itself would become a battleground. Pius did all he could to prevent this. In the first place, he decided that he himself would stay in Rome, knowing that his presence would be an effective way of dissuading the Allies from making a full-scale attack on the city. In this he was successful, but Rome was bombed several times. After two of the worst daylight raids, the Pope went in person to the parts of the city that had been bombed, prayed with the people and blessed the rescue-workers, and distributed cash from the Vatican funds to enable those who had lost their homes at least to buy food

and find shelter straight away. On 10 February 1944 Castel
Gandolfo was bombed, and about 500 of the refugees
sheltering there were killed. Pope Pius suffered greatly at
this, and sent protests to the Allies, though no one accepted
responsibility for the bombing. And on 15 February the
Allies bombed Monte Cassino, St Benedict's own abbey
where his body was buried, since they suspected it of being a
refuge for German troops or an ammunition store. Here too,
more than a hundred refugees were killed. The Pope
condemned this in no uncertain terms, though he learnt from
Abbot Diamare that, although there were no Germans and no
ammunition actually inside the abbey, the Germans had in
fact posted men and stored ammunition all around it. Later,
in 1947, he wrote a fairly brief encyclical letter, *"Fulgens
Radiatur"* ('he shines brilliantly') in praise of St Benedict,
expressing his deep sorrow that none of his urgent appeals
had been able to avert the destruction of the Abbey, and
appealing for contributions to rebuild Monte Cassino.

Rome freed

Rome was declared an open city in March, and in April the
Nazi commander announced that he would not defend it but
would retreat northwards before making a stand against the
Allied armies. The city was finally liberated on 2-4 June
1944 by the Allied forces. A Jewish Brigade Officer serving
in the US army was quoted in a Hebrew newspaper shortly
afterwards as saying, "When we entered Rome, the Jewish

survivors told us in a voice filled with deep gratitude and respect: 'If we have been rescued, if Jews are still alive in Rome, come with us and thank the Pope in the Vatican. For in the Vatican itself, in churches, monasteries and private homes, Jews were kept hidden at his personal orders.'"

General de Gaulle, leader of the Free French and later a French statesman and President, was received in audience by the Pope at the end of June 1944. He wrote afterwards in his war diaries: "Under the kindness of the welcome and the simplicity of the moment, I was struck by how sensible and powerful was his thinking. Pius XII judges everything from a perspective that surpasses human beings, their undertakings and their quarrels. But he knows what these cost them and he immediately suffers with all. One feels that the supernatural burden that he alone carries in the world weighs down his soul, but that he bears it willingly, certain of the end, sure of the way."

Relief work continues

Throughout all this time the Vatican's relief work in its own neighbourhood was growing steadily, as food supplies to Rome became smaller and smaller because of the fighting. By May 1944, the Vatican was supplying about 100,000 of the poor of Rome with daily meals at 1 lira a head. They also supplied the hospitals with food. Convoys of trucks went out into the Italian countryside to bring in food for all this at considerable risk, as they were often attacked by Allied aeroplanes by mistake for German munitions convoys, in spite of their Vatican markings.

At this stage the Pope was fighting a desperate battle through all the means at his command to help the Jews of Hungary and Slovakia, who were now being deported to concentration camps in large numbers. He appealed to the Regent of Hungary, Admiral Horthy, and for a while the persecution slackened in that country. However, in October that year Horthy himself was arrested, the Nazi group called the 'Arrow-Cross' took power, and the round-ups and deportations of Jews started up once again. The Pope was helped by the nuncios and bishops of Hungary and the surrounding countries, but again the proportion of Jewish men, women and children saved from the death camps was small in comparison with those who were captured and killed. Among Pope Pius's most effective helpers in rescuing the Jewish people in this part of Europe were Angelo Rotta, papal nuncio in Hungary, and Angelo Roncalli, apostolic delegate in Istanbul, Turkey, and later Pope John XXIII. Roncalli commented later, "In all these painful matters I have referred to the Holy See and simply carried out the Pope's orders: first and foremost to save Jewish lives." The Arrow-Cross regime lasted until February 1945. On 1 December 1944 the World Jewish Congress had already sent a telegram of thanks to the Holy See for the protection it gave under difficult conditions to the persecuted Jews in German-dominated Hungary.

PIUS XII - THE POST-WAR YEARS

Appeals for peace

As well as ensuring that the rescue and relief work continued, Pope Pius was doing his best to make the western democracies understand that true, lasting peace has to be based on justice and respect for human rights, not on building a distinction between the winners and losers of the war. He was strongly against the agreement reached between Churchill, Roosevelt and Stalin at Yalta in February 1945 on the division of Europe and Germany when the war ended. He foresaw that this would result in more harm and increasing injustice in coming years. He later said, "Do we have peace, true peace? No, merely a post-war period. How many years will it take to overcome the moral suffering? How much effort will it take to heal so many wounds? Today, as the reconstruction begins, mankind is beginning to realise how much care, honesty and charity will be required to rescue the world from physical and spiritual ruin, and to lead it back to the paths of peace and righteousness."

In April 1945 Pope Pius issued one of the first in a long series of encyclicals appealing for peace, and asking people all over the world to pray for it earnestly. What had been attained so far, as statesmen and historians later recognised, was not peace, but simply the absence of war and very soon, as the arms race between the United States and the Soviet Union began, the Cold War.

Four years before, in his radio message for Easter 1941 he had said, "In this tempest of misfortunes and perils, of afflictions and fears, our most powerful and safest haven of trust and peace is found in prayer to God, in whose hands rests not only the destiny of men but also the outcome of their most obdurate dissensions. Yes, let us pray for early peace. Let us pray for universal peace; not for peace based upon the oppression and destruction of peoples but peace which, while guaranteeing the honour of all nations, will satisfy their vital needs and insure the legitimate rights of all... peace that will be just, in accordance with human and Christian norms."

His message was still the same at the end of the war. "Change the heart, and the world will be changed. Root out greed and plant charity. Do you want peace? Do justice, and you will have peace. If therefore you desire to come to peace, do justice: avoid evil and do good. This is to love justice. And once you have avoided evil and done good, then seek peace and follow it." His personal motto as Pope was *Opus Iustitiae Pax* - "Peace is the work of justice."

Gratitude

As the war came to an end, expressions of gratitude reached the Pope and his representatives from Jewish individuals and organisations all over the world. Rabbi

Isaac Herzog, Chief Rabbi of Jerusalem, said, "The people of Israel will never forget what his Holiness and his illustrious delegates, inspired by the eternal principles of religion which form the very foundations of true civilisation, are doing for our unfortunate brothers and sisters in the most tragic hour of our history, which is living proof of divine Providence in this world."

Dr Joseph Nathan, representing the Hebrew Commission said, addressing the Jewish Community in September 1945, "We express our heartfelt gratitude to those who protected and saved us during the Nazi-Fascist persecutions. Above all, we acknowledge the Supreme Pontiff and the religious men and women who, executing the directives of the Holy Father, recognised the persecuted as their brothers and with great abnegation, hastened to help them, disregarding the terrible dangers to which they were exposed." On 12 October 1945 the World Jewish Congress sent a gift of 2 million lire to the Vatican. Israel's second Prime Minister, Moshe Sharett, later told the Pope that his "first duty was to thank him and the Catholic Church for all they had done to rescue Jews."

The Chief Rabbi of Rome, Dr Israel Zolli, became a Catholic after the war. He was convinced of the truth of Catholicism by his own study, helped by God's grace and the example he had seen set by Catholics during the war. In tribute to the Pope he took the baptismal name of Eugenio.

In 1955 the Israeli Philharmonic Orchestra, on its first European tour, gave a performance in the Vatican in honour of Pius XII, playing one of Beethoven's symphonies in the Consistory Hall as a mark of the lasting gratitude of the Israeli people for the help given them by the Pope and Catholics throughout Nazi-occupied Europe during the war.

Children after the war

Characteristically, amidst all the complications and hard work which the end of the war brought with it, the Pope's abiding concern was for the children who had been left destitute by the war. He was already doing all he could to help them with the means at his disposal. He knew that this was not enough to meet all the needs. On 6 January 1946 he issued a short encyclical letter (*Quemadmodum*) to Catholic bishops around the world. He asked them to pass on to all the faithful of their dioceses, first of all a call to prayer, and secondly an appeal to their charity to give as much money as they could to this cause and help in any other possible way. He spoke in moving words of the sufferings of abandoned children and the dangers they were exposed to, as something that was very close to his heart, and constantly before his mind's eye. The relief work done by the Vatican - mainly the distribution of free meals, but also clothes, blankets and medicines - for the poor of Rome and Italy continued throughout 1945, 1946 and well into 1947, with the Pope mobilising all possible resources for it.

Pope Pius XII.

Mediator Dei

In November 1947 came the publication of Pope Pius's encyclical *Mediator Dei* ('Mediator of God') about the sacred liturgy. He loved the liturgy as the perfect expression of the worship offered to God by the Mystical Body of Christ, and, like Popes before and after him, he wanted the Church to enrich the way the liturgy was carried out. At the same time, he wanted all Catholics to be aware that the whole point of the liturgy was prayer and adoration; to prevent the external rites and ceremonies and singing from being separated from, or indeed replacing, personal prayer, but instead to make them the expression and enrichment of prayer. This was a long-standing concern, shown again in his encyclical letter *Musicae Sacrae Disciplina* (On Sacred Music) dated 25 December 1955.

The struggle against Communism

What Pope Pius had foreseen from Communism very soon came true. In the eastern bloc countries, behind the 'iron curtain' which now divided Europe, the Communist governments made the practice of religion more and more difficult, and the spread of it nearly impossible. Where they met determined resistance they reacted savagely, as in the case of Cardinal Joszef Mindszenty of Hungary, who was arrested, brainwashed, submitted to a show trial, and imprisoned, in the winter of 1948-9. Pope Pius denounced the whole procedure publicly. He called a special assembly of the Sacred Consistory of Cardinals to discuss the Church's approach to the persecution of the Church in Eastern Europe.

He suffered personally with those who were suffering because of religion, as much as he had suffered for the victims of the war. At the same time, he was aware of the very real danger that Communism would spread in Western Europe, starting in Italy itself with the 1948 elections which Communists were widely predicted to win. He spoke, as usual, not about politics but about the truths of man, society and God, and he made sure that everyone in Italy could hear or read what he had to say. The Communists were defeated at the election, partly at least thanks to the Pope's words and prayers.

1948 was also a time of particular difficulty in Palestine, where the newly-created state of Israel had been immediately plunged into war with its neighbours. Pope Pius never ceased to pray and ask for prayers for peace in the Holy Land and a real solution to the problems there.

Jubilee

In 1950 the whole Church celebrated a Holy Year for the Jubilee Year of the Redemption. In his 1949 Christmas Message at the solemn opening of the Holy Year, Pope Pius appealed to all Catholics to besiege heaven with continuous prayers throughout the year for the sanctification of souls through prayer and penance and through devotion to Christ and the Church; for world peace and the protection of the Holy Places; for the defence of the Church against the attacks of her enemies and the return of unbelievers to Christ; and for social justice and charity for those in want. He was ambitious to make this a really holy year for all Catholics, conscious of how much good they could achieve in the present situation of the world if they followed the commands of Christ in all their fullness. Throughout the year he took special care to see that pilgrims were properly catered for in Rome, and he received a total of almost three million people, holding large public audiences three or four times a week and smaller ones every day. He always loved the contact with ordinary people, whether Catholics or not, offered by these audiences. People used to confide all sorts of things to him as he went around and greeted them. It was not unknown for someone to tell him that they would like to go to Confession. The Pope would promptly take the person aside and hear his Confession there and then. At one audience, someone brought a white skullcap and asked Pope Pius to exchange it for his own, which he did, laughing. Realising how much the skullcap of the Vicar of Christ was prized by families and parishes, he then adopted the habit of using a new skullcap about twenty times in one audience. As each one was handed to him from the crowds, he would place it on his head, wear it for a few minutes, and then return it.

Developing Catholic teaching

In August he published one of his most famous encyclicals, *Humani Generis,* on "False Trends in Modern Teaching". Convinced as always that the solution to many problems is a fuller and deeper knowledge and understanding of the truth of Christ, the Pope gave clear pointers to enable people to appreciate the value of what had always been taught by the Church, and to enable teachers and scholars to explore new fields of knowledge confidently and fruitfully, without being misled by current fads or popular misconceptions.

On 1 November Pope Pius, whose love for Our Lady was, if anything, progressively deeper as time went on, solemnly proclaimed that Our Lady's bodily assumption into heaven at the end of her earthly life was a truth that was to be believed by all Catholics. He had previously prayed about this for years, had commissioned a special theological study of the subject, and had consulted all the bishops of the Catholic Church before making this declaration. It was no new idea, since the Assumption of our Lady into Heaven had long been celebrated by the Church in its liturgy and was one of the mysteries of the rosary. Pope Pius simply established this truth as part of the faith of the Church for all time, and developed the theology around it.

The end of the year was saddened by the outbreak of the Korean War, to which the Pope reacted, as always, with yet more faith and prayer.

The Pope and the World

In spite of all that he had heard about and witnessed before, during and after the Second World War, Pope Pius never looked on anyone as an enemy. His 1944 Christmas message had made this clear. Concerning individuals who had "taken advantage of the war to commit real and proven crimes against the laws common to all peoples, crimes for which supposed military necessity may have afforded a pretext but could never offer an excuse - no-one, certainly, will wish to disarm justice in their regard. ... But only those individuals who were guilty of such offences should be punished; not whole communities." As has been noted above, he did not regard the Russian people as enemies either, although they were controlled by a ruthless Communist regime. He always prayed and appealed for prayers for unbelievers to find their way to the truth, and did what he could - however little or hopeless it appeared - to hold out the hand of friendship. By the early 1950s it was clear to everyone that the Communists were pressing on with their objective of rooting out all religious practice in the countries under their rule. On 7 July 1952 the Pope wrote an Apostolic Letter addressed to "the dearly beloved peoples of Russia", saying how much he prayed for them "to enjoy, together with a just and reasonable material prosperity, that freedom also through which every one of you may be able to safeguard your human dignity, to know the teachings of the true religion and to give due worship to God not only in the inner sanctuary of your own conscience but also openly, in public and private life." He added, "If some people, deceived by lies and calumnies, are openly opposed to us, so all the greater is our pity and all the warmer is our love."

His concern for all the countries of Eastern Europe and the Far East grew steadily during the post-war years. He knew that in China particularly, people were being imprisoned, tortured and killed for their loyalty to the Roman Catholic Church. He addressed several Apostolic Letters and encyclicals to the Catholics in China, although some of these messages were prevented from reaching them and others were allowed to be published in China only in a very distorted form.

Hungary was again in the forefront of his concern in late 1956, when a popular attempt to overthrow the Communist regime was crushed by force with Soviet tanks. As usual, the Pope's weapons were his prayers and words, together with the prayers of Christians around the world. He also ensured that refugees fleeing Hungary after the crushing of the uprising were given aid and support.

Technology and society

The Pope declared that 1954 would be a Marian Year, to honour the centenary of the definition of the dogma of the Immaculate Conception. In the course of it, the Pope became seriously ill, but overcame his weakness sufficiently to canonise Pope Pius X (whom he had beatified in 1951) on 29 May. He continued to write, publishing four encyclicals and many addresses, including an important one on the subject of television, which was already widespread in affluent countries. He pointed out that television was a great gift of science which could bring families together and broaden their minds and outlook, but that there was a real danger that it could also bring disruption and quarrels into the home, and harm people's minds, especially children's.

He was always closely interested in the progress of every field of science, saying that "Scientific knowledge has its own value, a value existing quite independently of the usefulness or use of the acquired knowledge. Moreover, knowledge as such and the full understanding of any truth raise no moral objection. By virtue of this principle, research and the acquisition of truth for arriving at new, wider and deeper knowledge and understanding of the same truth are in themselves in accordance with the moral order. But this does not mean that all methods, or any single method, arrived at by scientific and technical research offers every moral guarantee. Nor, moreover, does it mean that every method becomes licit simply because it increases and deepens our knowledge." He thought and prayed deeply, as always, on the fundamental relationship between scientific research and the eternal truths, and provided important guidelines to help scientists in their pursuit of truth, and to enable them to see their responsibility to humanity in all its aspects.

He was particularly active in the field of medical ethics, when doctors, surgeons and others engaged in the care of the sick would send their questions and doubts for him to consider and resolve in the light of faith. In an address given on 14 September 1952 on "The moral limits of medical research and treatment", (from which the quotation in the previous paragraph is taken) he set out the moral principles on which medical research must be based, as guidelines which researchers could use to evaluate their own approach. He was always concerned that people should see such principles as something constructive and positive, and he concluded his address by saying, "The great moral demands force the impetuous flow of human thought to run, like water from the mountains, into certain channels. They contain the flow to increase its efficiency and usefulness. They dam it so that it does not overflow and cause ravages that can never be compensated for by the special good it seeks. In appearance, moral demands are a brake; but in fact they contribute to the best and most beautiful of what man has produced for science, the individual and the community."

Nuclear power

Nuclear power had been developed in the 1940s and used by the Allies to bring the war with Japan to an end. The Pope was fully aware of all the possibilities and dangers that it represented. In 1957 the Japanese Prime Minister Nobosuke Kishi sent a representative to ask the Pope for support in seeking the abolition of nuclear and atomic weapons. In the previous sixteen years the Pope had spoken and written about the possible scope of atomic and nuclear energy, and the moral questions raised, at least nine times, and had appealed that the new developments should be placed at the service of peace, not used for war and destruction. He had also explained, through the example of the great non-Catholic scientist Max Planck, how the study of the atom leads one to recognise the existence of a personal God.

Messages to the laity

Pope Pius was also deeply concerned about the day-to-day practice of the faith among all Catholics, and did all he could to help them to live in a way that was consistent with what they believed. For example, in a document dated 5 October 1957 on "The Lay Apostolate", he wrote: "We would like to draw your attention most especially to one aspect of the education of young Catholics: the formation of their apostolic spirit. Instead of giving way to a rather selfish tendency, thinking only of the salvation of their own souls, they should become aware of their responsibilities towards others and of the means of helping them". Further on in the same document, speaking of the Christian spirit in the workplace, he said:

"Wherever it is active it will create the right atmosphere, will exercise a good influence, and radiate a new conception of life. Thus, for example, a Catholic foreman will interest himself in the newcomers, find them proper lodgings, help them to make good friends, put them in contact with the local life of the Church, and will help them to adapt themselves easily to their new situation."

Many years previously, on 26 October 1941, he had received a group of women from Catholic Action in Italy. His words to them, later published as the allocution *Davanti a Questa,* helped them to understand more fully how important the task of a woman was, both during the war and in general. Among other things, he told them: "It is a curious circumstance and, as Pope Pius XI remarked in his encyclical, a lamentable one, that whereas no one would dream of suddenly becoming a mechanic or an engineer, a doctor or a lawyer, without any apprenticeship or preparation, yet every day there are numbers of young men and women who marry without having given an instant's thought to preparing themselves for the arduous work of educating their children." (Pius XI's encyclical *Divini Illius Magistri,* on the Christian Education of Youth, was published on 31 December 1929.) In speaking of the growth and development of little children, his great love for them was apparent in the tenderness and sensitivity of his words. He went on, "Train the minds of your children. Do not give them wrong ideas or wrong reasons for things; whatever their questions may be, do not answer them with evasions or untrue statements, which their minds rarely accept; but take occasion from them lovingly and patiently to train their minds, which want only to open to the truth and to grasp it."

Death of Pope Pius XII

On 9 October 1958 Pope Pius died, aged 82. Because of the enormous reputation he had acquired during the nineteen eventful years of his pontificate, much of the world joined in mourning him, and messages of condolence poured into the Vatican. Dr William F. Rosenblum in his sermon in Temple Israel, New York, 12 October 1958, paid tribute to the Pope as "a great religious leader whose works for brotherliness and peace in a time of crisis in our history should remain as an example to emulate." Before beginning a concert of the New York Philharmonic Orchestra, conductor Leonard Bernstein called for a minute's silence in memory of Pope Pius XII, "a very great man." These are just two examples out of very many; no other Pope in history had been so universally praised by Jewish people, both during his lifetime and at his death.

Posthumous attacks on Pius XII

However, five years later public perception of Pope Pius XII began to change. 1963 saw the production of a long play by Rolf Hochhuth, a German playwright, called *Der Stellvertreter,* variously translated into English as *The*

Deputy, The Vicar or *The Representative*. Set in the
Second World War, the plot was based around a German
SS officer, Kurt Gerstein, who had really existed, and a
fictional Jesuit priest, Ricardo Fontana. It also featured
Pope Pius XII, showing him in total contrast to the truth
as an icy-cold, detached figure who did not want to know
about the fate of the Jews in the Holocaust, and refused to
denounce the Nazis partly out of moral cowardice and
partly because he was afraid of damaging the Vatican's
supposed 'financial interests' abroad.

From the start of the cold war, Communist
propagandists had made a point of accusing the Catholic
Church and the members of its hierarchy of having
collaborated with Hitler during the Second World War
out of an obsessive fear of Communism. Several bishops
and churchmen in Eastern European countries had been
put on trial. Pope Pius, who stood firmly against atheistic
Communism, came under special attack in retrospect,
even though during the actual war, the weekly publication
of the Communist International had called him "the
leader of the Catholic resistance movement" against the
Nazis. In the 1960s the Communists' new image of Pope
Pius was taken up by Western historians and academics.

From that time on, attacks against Pope Pius XII's
'silence' have continued and worsened, some reaching
the point of declaring that he was pro-Nazi and anti-
Semitic himself. These allegations may be the result of

complete ignorance of the facts of Pope Pius's life, or else of the writers' hidden agendas. Many true events are misrepresented, mixed with untruths and presented in the worst light imaginable, and only a knowledge of the real facts of the case can give the true picture.

Pius XII himself, and his supporters at the time, said that if he publicly denounced the killing of Jews by the Nazis, the situation in Germany would have become much worse, Jews all over occupied Europe would have suffered even more than they did, and many more of them would have been killed. This was his reason for not speaking out, and is based on knowledge of the actual way Hitler behaved - any criticism of Hitler and any act against him brought about very heavy reprisals. Critics of Pius XII say that if he had spoken out, German Catholics would have stopped supporting the Nazis, and the Holocaust of the Jews would have been halted. This is pure supposition and has no foundation in reality.

One of those who knew the truth about Pope Pius XII was the British envoy to the Holy See during the war, Francis d'Arcy Osborne, who, with other Allied diplomats, had been obliged to live in the Vatican itself for most of the war and had come to know Pope Pius well. When Hochhuth's play was first produced, he wrote in a letter to the newspapers, "Pius XII was the most warmly humane, kindly, generous, sympathetic (and, incidentally, saintly) character that it has been my privilege to meet in the course of a long life. I know his sensitive nature was acutely and incessantly alive to the tragic volume of human suffering caused by the War and, without the slightest doubt, he would have been ready and glad to give his life to redeem humanity from its consequences." Proceedings for Pope Pius XII's beatification were begun by Pope Paul VI in 1964.

Bibliography

Pierre Blet, *Pius XII and the Second World War according to the Vatican Archives,* (trans. Lawrence Johnson), Gracewing, 1999

Dimitri Cavalli, *"The Commission that couldn't shoot straight",* *New Oxford Review,* July/August 2002; http://www.ewtn.com/library/issues/cmmssP12.htm

Owen Chadwick, *Britain and the Vatican during the Second World War,* Cambridge University Press, 1986

Camille M. Cianfarra, *The War and the Vatican,* Burns Oates & Washbourne Ltd, 1945

Rabbi David Dalin, Ph.D., *"A Righteous Gentile: Pope Pius XII and the Jews",* http://www.catholicleague.org/pius/dalin.htm

Robert A. Graham, *Pius XII's Defense of Jews and Others 1944-45 in Pius XII and the Holocaust: A Reader* (ed. Virgil C. Blum), Catholic League Publications (Milwaukee), 1988

Peter Gumpel, *"Pius XII as he really was",* *The Tablet,* 13 February 1999

Leo J. Haigerty (editor), *Pius XII and Technology,* The Bruce Publishing Company, 1962

Alden Hatch and Seamus Walshe, *Crown of Glory: the life of Pope Pius XII,* Heinemann, 1957

Pinchas Lapide, *The Last Three Popes and the Jews,* Hawthorn Press and Souvenir Press, 1967 (also published as *Three Popes and the Jews*)

Margherita Marchione, *Yours is a Precious Witness: memoirs of Jews and Catholics in wartime Italy,* Paulist Press, 1997

Margherita Marchione, *Pope Pius XII, Architect for Peace,* Gracewing, 2000

Margherita Marchione, *Consensus and Controversy: Defending Pope Pius XII,* Paulist Press, 2002

Margherita Marchione, *"The Truth and Pope Pius XII",* *Homiletic and Pastoral Review,* November 2002, pp. 62-66

Mary Ball Martinez, *"Pope Pius XII in the Second World War"*, Institute for Historical Review, on website http://marynet.com/piusxii.html

Michael Marrus, review essay *"The Vatican on Racism and Anti-Semitism, 1938-1939: a new look at a might-have-been"*, in Holocaust and Genocide Studies vol. 11, no. 3, Winter 1997, pp. 378-395

Ralph McInerny, *The Defamation of Pius XII,* St Augustine's Press, 2001

Pope Pius XI, encyclicals:
    Mit brennender Sorge, 14 March 1937
    Divini Redemptoris, 19 March 1937

Pope Pius XII, encyclicals:
    Summi Pontificatus, 20 October 1939
    Mystici Corporis Christi, 29 June 1943
    Divino Afflante Spiritu, 30 September 1943
    Quemadmodum, 6 January 1946
    Mediator Dei, 20 November 1947

Maurice Quinlan (editor) *Guide for Living: a selection of letters and addresses of His Holiness Pope Pius XII,* Evans Brothers Ltd, 1958

Charles Rankin, *The Pope Speaks,* The Catholic Book Club, 1941

Mark Riebling, *"Pius XII: Was the Pope a Nazi?",* http://www.markriebling.com/nazipope.html

Ronald J. Rychlak, *Hitler, the War and the Pope,* Genesis Press, 2000

Jan Olav Smit, *Pope Pius XII,* Burns Oates & Washbourne Ltd, 1951

"A message from the Apostolic Delegate" [Archbishop Godfrey], *The Tablet,* CLXXIII, p. 311 (11 March, 1939)

Vatican Commission for Religious Relations with the Jews, *We Remember: a Reflection on the Shoah,* Libreria Editrice Vaticana, 1998